THE

 TO

BOOK OF

TURTLE ISLAND

By Michael P. Earney

ISBN-13:   978-1-941345-89-4   HB
ISBN-13:   978-1-941345-90-0   PB

ERIN GO BRAGH
Publishing

Canyon Lake, TX
www.ErinGoBraghPublishing.com

ACKNOWLEDGEMENTS

My thanks to those members of the Turtle Island Nations
that I have had the pleasure to know and from whom I have learned.

During the years I lived in New Mexico the proximity of the Pueblos there allowed me the opportunity to visit and attend some of their celebrations. My film work gave me closer access to the Native American, (in Navajoland I was knocked down and stepped on by a galloping horse and rider while filming a rodeo.) I was the sound recordist for the southwest leg of His Holiness the Karmapa's US tour. The Hopi performed a special rain ceremony for His Holiness. The ceremony was performed because there had been no rain for some time prior to his visit. A storm arose during the ceremony and rain fell in torrents. I was editor and co-producer on, *Look what we've done to this land* a film about strip mining on the Hopi and Navajo reservations. In 1977 I was director and editor for *Make me Wise* a documentary on the innovative inclusion of Indian educators in Indian schools, that took me to a number of reservations and Indian communities around the country. In respect to the fact that these experiences may have contributed to the way in which I have approached the subject here, I can only give my thanks for the events and the people I came into contact with in the process.

I want to thank Barbara Baggett for her invaluable help in the editing process
and to Kathleen J. Shields for her tireless work bringing the book to completion.

DISCLAIMER

The information in this book is accurate to the best of the authors' knowledge. It is intended for educational purposes only. Images acquired through various means, fair use, no copyright infringement is intended.

THIS LAND

In 14 hundred and 92 Columbus sailed the ocean blue.
And what did he find for me and for you?

America! This great land of the free
named for Americo Vespucci.
He was the one who called, 'Land Ho!
To the cheers of all on the deck below.

However, long before Columbus came,
America had another name.
For the People watching on the shore
Turtle Island was the name it bore.

Yet, before these folk could have their say,
their lives and ways were swept away
Disease and warfare thinned their ranks.
For which, the settlers gave god thanks.

They then went on to build a nation.
And, though seldom in the best location,
some tribes got a reservation,
(where you can go when on vacation).

Accepting those that have a different way of life
put an end to all that mindless strife.
Still, it really does seem rather odd,
to say that we're one people under god.

Michael P. Earney July, 2020

Introduction

Author note: I am fully aware that setting out to write this book is rather like wandering into a minefield. I am not a Native American, I'm not an expert, (on anything) but I am curious and have not shied away from tackling subjects I know nothing about. This volume may present more obstacles than some others, not the least because I know most Native Americans will not take kindly to a non-native presuming to write on the subject. Even the use of the term, Native American offends many. Redskin, Indian, even more offensive. Aboriginal, how does that go down? As I said, it's a minefield but, here goes. As with all histories the story varies from source to source. I have researched as many as I could and have tried to bring together the information in as coherent and intelligible way as possible while dealing with thousands of years of history. I apologize for omitting events that might seem of paramount importance to some while trying to convey as much information as possible in the limited space this format demands. By the same token I have limited the scope to cover only those indigenous people that occupied or occupy what is now the United States.

Most aboriginal peoples of the Americas share the common features of natives of Mongolia, Siberia and the Far East suggesting that the earliest settlers crossed a land bridge where the Bering Strait now lies. This is estimated to have begun around 65,000 yrs. ago when nomadic people of the area simply extended their hunting ranges over a long period of time into what became, as sea levels rose, a separate continent. Finds in California suggest that Neanderthals or some other tool wielding species, were feeding on Mastodons there 130,000 yrs. ago. This is hotly contested by some archaeologists, a species that find it hard to agree about much when it comes to dating of archaeological sites. There are widely varying dates offered for the arrival of humans, from 250,000 to 30,000 yrs. and the search goes on. Over the following eons this spread continued until the continent was occupied from the farthest north down to Tierra del Fuego at the southern tip and from west to east. It is likely that some contact continued, the strait was not that difficult to cross, and there is disputed evidence, of later contacts from other parts of the world. The ocean currents that allowed the old world to discover the new world could just as easily take the large whaling canoes of the north and Mayan trading ships to the old world. There is tantalizing evidence that such trips did occur. Theories abound. We know that the extensive trade routes that covered the land allowed for the transmission of ideas and skills to be passed along. Still, the isolation was enough that beasts of burden, other than dogs, the wheel and other advances in knowledge and skills, did not make their way here. Christopher Columbus never set foot on the continent, he stopped at the islands in the Caribbean, but he set off the stream of Europeans who wanted nothing more than to exploit the land and all that it contained. Throughout the history of the discovery and occupation of North, Central and South America, relations between Europeans and natives were sometimes friendly but generally combative, ultimately resulting in the subjugation or extinction of the natives. It is not known how many tribes or people there were on the continent when the Europeans arrived, a hundred million people by some estimates. Infectious diseases that arrived with the invaders, for which the native people had no immunity, spread across the land wiping out entire tribes before they even saw their nemesis. Malaria, from mosquitoes brought from abroad, along with other mosquito borne diseases, is estimated to have killed ninety-five million. The Church, which wanted its share, at first couldn't decide whether they were dealing with human beings, making the genocide easier, although later, sometimes too late, it was priests that set their converts to record aspects of the past and were responsible for the preservation, as well as the destruction, of much of what is known about the natives. Seeing the mass destruction and loss of important material, they collected much of what remains. In Texas, Mirabeau Lamar who succeeded Sam Houston as governor, called for the total extinct or expulsion of all Indians in the Republic, that was in 1838. His words were echoed across the country. Today, tribal people in Brazil are still being evicted and exterminated as they fight to protect their land from illegal gold-mining, logging, polluting oil exploration and settlers. Confrontations between government and tribes continue to occur in numerous Latin American countries.

Throughout the United States Native Americans still fight for recognition. Depending on who you ask there are 562, 573 or 574 Federally recognized tribes at this time, many unrecognized tribes and groups with no tribal affiliation. The Esselen Tribe of California who inhabited the Santa Lucia Mountains and Big Sur coastline for thousands of years were landless for hundreds of years until May 2nd. 2020. With the help of Western Rivers Conservancy they got nearly 1,200 acres of their sacred land back. Such struggles are enacting throughout the country year in, year out. Here as elsewhere, art and artifacts created by indigenous artists and craftsmen/women are eagerly sought for in market places and on reservations. Artists that no longer have any tribal affiliation sell their work in stores and galleries. The Santa Fe, New Mexico Indian Market that has taken place annually for ninety nine years, draws crowds of a 150,000 from around the world. A 1000 artists from 200 federally recognized tribes in the US and Canada exhibit there over two days. The traditional arts such as, basketry, jewelry, weaving and pottery remain favorites along with most other art forms including song and dance. All this while many native people live in poverty, reservations are without electricity or running water, those that live off the reservation are often discriminated against and suffer from mental and physical ill health. Trying to condense thousands of years of history into short essays has its drawbacks but I hope to at least give some idea of the complex and fascinating gifts that we have received from the original occupants of Turtle Island.

Creation stories abound, almost every tribe claimed to be the original or the first people. The Great Spirit having brought them into being and endowed them with the task of maintaining the balance of nature and of living in harmony with it. For thousands of years that is exactly what they did, most tribal declarations express the desire to restore that balance. Whether such a goal is achievable given the structure of our societies, is hard to conceive. Utilization and exploitation at the expense of nature is more the norm. Through every form of travail, the Native American has persevered; perhaps their philosophy will someday prevail.

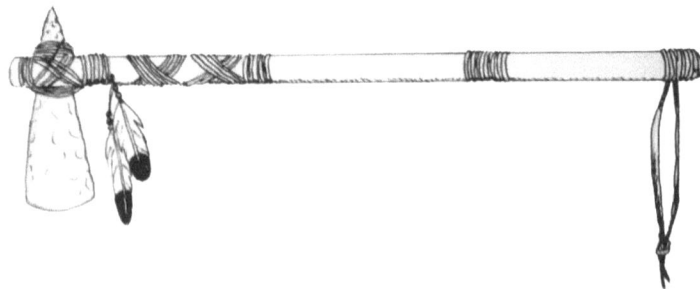

Bannerstones

Hundreds of well sculpted stone objects, in a wide variety of shapes and sizes and types of stone, have been found throughout the United States by archaeologists. These objects became known as bannerstones. What the purpose of the stones might have been was unknown. In 1930 archaeologist William Webb determined that they had been attached to a spear in order to increase its velocity and force. For thousands of years before the bow and arrow were introduced, the atlatl, a hinged throwing stick upon which a spear was laid, served as the weapon of choice for hunting and warfare. Webb was convinced that the bannerstone was made for these spears. Unfortunately, those that tried out the idea were unable to confirm that they helped in anyway. In 1983 another archaeologist, Larry Kinsella, after much study and trials, concluded that the bannerstones were attached to the back end of the atlatl itself to act as a counterbalance to the spearhead. This measure eased the strain while the hunter, with his atlatl drawn back, waited for the right moment to fire. Less strain, more accuracy. This is now the generally accepted explanation for these unique objects. However, no bannerstones have been found that date after 1500BCE even though the atlatl continued in use for another two millenia. Either they no longer served a practical or ceremonial purpose or perhaps, some dating from that period are still waiting to be found; alternatively, someone will yet come up with another explanation for the bannerstone.

ANASAZI

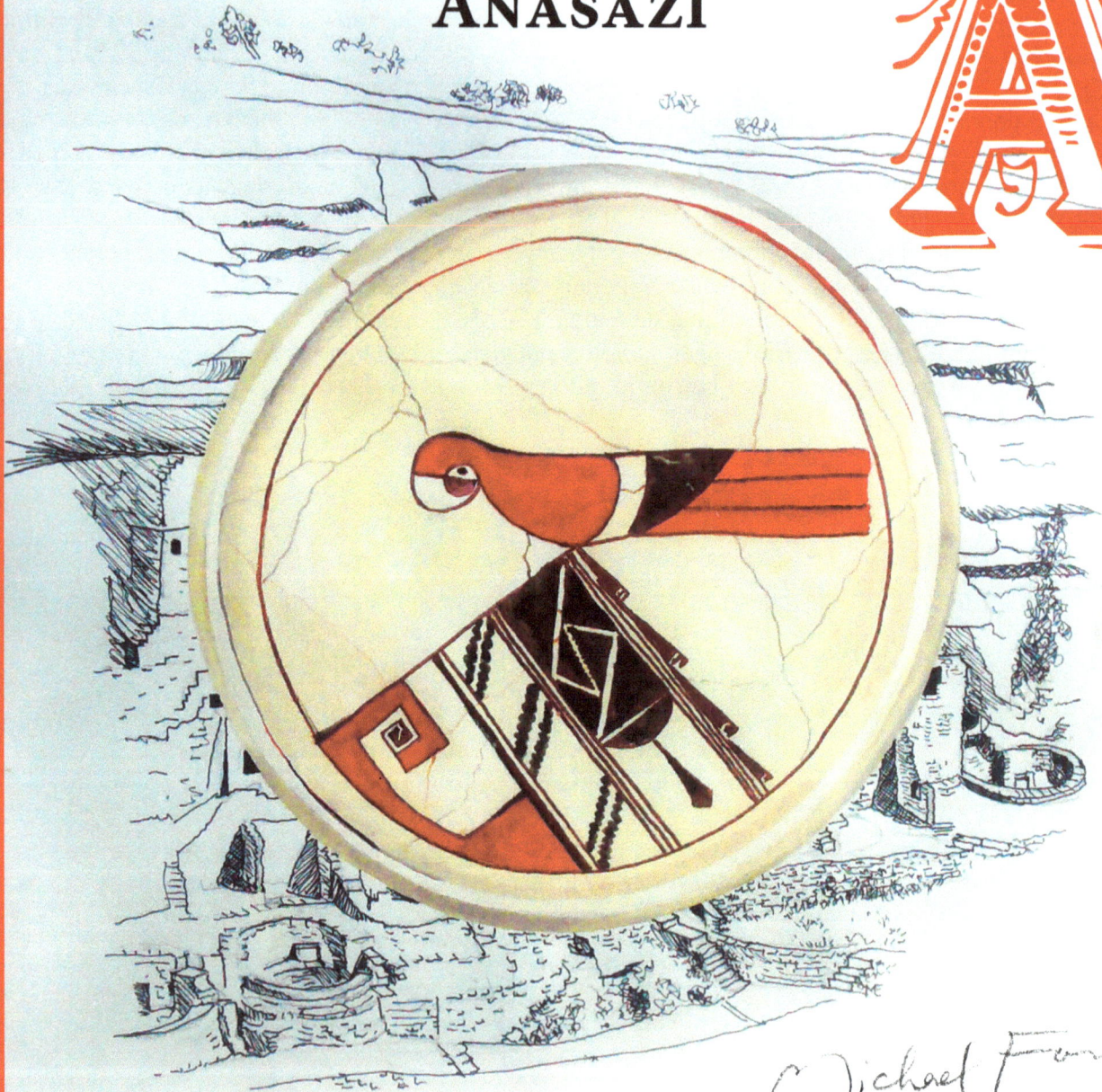

Michael Ferrin

A Is for Anasazi

The Anasazi people are renowned for their basketry and pottery though they are mostly known for the magnificent and numerous ruins that are all that remain of their pueblos and cliff cities found throughout the Four Corners area of Arizona, Colorado, Utah and New Mexico. The Mogollan and Hohokam people who lived in the area for more than a thousand years were slowly absorbed or displaced by these Desert Wanderers/hunters arriving from the north. From where exactly, is unknown. The history of the people, who came to be known as the Anasazi, is broken up into two periods, Basketmaker, and Pueblo. Around 1 CE the Basketmakers were sufficiently settled to be producing their finely woven baskets, some of which survive until today. They were involved in agriculture, growing a simple form of corn. Just like their predecessors, the Mogollan and the Hohokam, they had trade and cultural ties with the Toltec and Aztec people of Mexico. The Sun Dagger petroglyph at Chaco, one of many pictographs and petroglyphs they created, shows that they studied the sky. Archaeological study shows hundreds of years of matrilineal descent, a practice seen in some tribes today. As time passed they began to live in pit-dwellings with slab linings, an improvement on the simple pit-dwellings of the people they displaced. Beans and newer forms of corn, probably imported from Mexico, made life easier and the development of their own distinctive pottery led to the Pueblo period. Structures of adobe brick and simple wattle-and-daub homes started to be built around 700 CE. Villages grew in size in and around the fertile valleys and canyons where they farmed. As the population grew these villages with their now multi-storied dwellings and large *Kivas;* circular, underground rooms where religious ceremonies, open only to clan members, were carried out, like we see in the Pueblos of today, must have started to take up vital farming land, for cliff-dwellings, first built into natural caves, started to climb the steep walls of the hills surrounding the valleys. These cliff-dwellings mostly reserved for the elite, that now attract thousands of tourists each year, also served as protection from the Athapaskan groups who had begun to infiltrate the area. Over a period of a thousand years the Anasazi nation had grown to the point where their many crops now included cotton, their outside contacts and trade relations provided exotic materials like turquoise, shells from the Gulf of Mexico and other distant places, from which they fashioned fine jewelry. Their pottery designs and forms were influenced by works as far away as California and the Southeast. A complex network of roads, some of them wide and well-engineered, stretched many miles linking multiple population centers and trade sources. Climate change, many years of drought, invasion, over exploitation of resources, religious disputes, all have been offered as the cause for the collapse of this civilization. Intercommunal violence that included cannibalism also occurred perhaps set off by the impact of those other events. Whatever the cause, the Anasazi, like the people they displaced, dispersed into the surrounding landscape spreading far and wide. The Puebloans of the Rio Grande valley and elsewhere trace their ancestry to the Anasazi. The influence of this civilization on peoples throughout the southwest cannot be over emphasized.

Cool Fact: The Navaho, who moved into the area many years later, determined that the long abandoned ruins had been built by the Anasazi, variously translated as; "Ancient enemy", "Enemy of our Ancestors" or the now preferred, "The Ancient Ones." Although some still take exception to its use, it remains the name by which they are known.

What other Tribal names start with A?

BLACKFOOT

B is for Blackfoot

The Niitsitapii, "Real People" or, "Original People" are a group of tribes called the Siksika, Kainai or Kainah, the Northern and Southern Piikani. Only one of the tribes are called Blackfoot. These Plains Indians were nomadic hunter/gathers occupying a large territory stretching from the North Saskatchewan river in Canada to the Missouri river in Montana. As with all hunter/gathers their lives and activities followed the seasons but central to their ways was the buffalo. Following the Buffalo with their tipis and their dog drawn *travois,* the Blackfoot devised ways to hunt them for food and virtually every other use they could find. Buffalo skins were used for clothing and cover for their tipis along with other animal hides, tools and weapons were made from their bones, soap was made from their fat, tendons and sinew were used to tie everything that needed tying. The stomach and bladder were cleaned and prepared for use as containers for liquids, dried dung was used for fuel. The Blackfoot considered the buffalo sacred. Midsummer was the occasion for the Sun Dance a ten-day event and the only time all 4 nations assembled as one. This was also the time when the Chokecherry ripened, it, with other fruits, dried meat and buffalo fat was made into pemmican by the women to provide for the winter and when hunting was poor. The introduction of the horse in the 18th century radically changed the lives of the Blackfoot. They could now travel faster and farther becoming the most powerful of all the Plains tribes and earning the name, "The Lords of the Plains". The horse became a measure of wealth. An individual's prestige was based upon the amount of horses he could give away, similar to the 'potlatch' of the Alaskan people. Stealing horses became a way of life. Along with the horse came guns. Wars between the tribes took on a character of its own, being a warrior was a rite of passage, elevating one's social rank. It also led to fractious interaction with settlers. Trade between the Blackfoot and companies in the fur trade began in the mid-eighteenth century but competition with fur trappers was hostile early on. George Catlin, who spent some time with the Blackfoot, said this about the relationship of the Blackfoot and the American Fur Company; *"- the Company lose some fifteen to twenty men annually to these people in defense of what they deem their property and their rights. Trinkets and whiskey, however, will soon spread their charms amongst these, as they have among other tribes; and white man's voracity will sweep the prairies and the streams of their wealth, to the Rocky Mountains and the Pacific Ocean; leaving the Indians to inhabit, and at last to starve upon, a dreary and solitary waste."* Competition grew on all fronts, the slaughter of the bison became an industry, both for meat and as a means to open more land for settlement and as a way to control the plains tribesmen. Depriving them of their way of life gave the government control where they could live. Diseases to which the natives had no immunity killed thousands; this and all the other pressures ended their dominance of the Plains. Forced onto reservations, one tribe settled in Northwest Montana, the other three of the confederacy live in Canada. After many years of hardship the People settled into farming, ranching and light industry. Long suppressed, they have revived their language and Lifeways. The Sun Dance is once again celebrated in midsummer; pride in their place in the history of the Americas is displayed throughout the reservation.

Cool Fact: Of the once wide variety of dogs that came from Asia with the people only seven breeds remain. These include the Malamute, the Chihuahua and the Carolina dog that is still living wild in South Carolina and Georgia. The fur of the Salish Wool dog, now extinct, provided "wool" which was woven into blankets. Dogs helped with hunting as well as pulling peoples' belongings on the *travois*. They also served as food in hard times. They interbred with Coyotes and were killed along with their owners by imported diseases.

What other Tribal names start with B?

CADDO

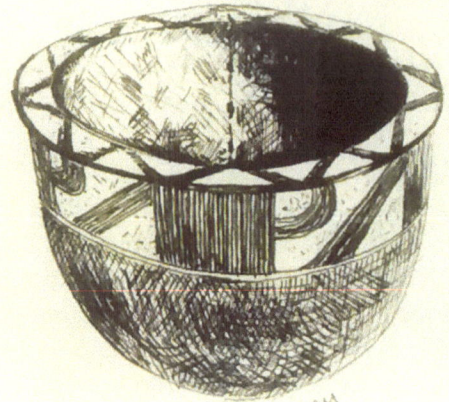

Earney

Earney

Michael Earney

C is for Caddo

Caddo early history, like most of the pre-contact history of American Indian tribes, is lost. However, the Caddo deserve a place in the history of Texas for many reasons, not the least of which is the fact that they may have arrived by sea. At the very least, culturally, they were heir to advances coming from the south. Their ceremonial centers, dominated by large temple mounds, link them to the civilizations of what is now Mexico and Central America. Sometime before 500CE, along the Gulf coast a culturally advanced people settled and spread. Most of the Gulf coast of Texas was already occupied by the Karankawa, so the Caddo, as part of what is known as the Mississippi pattern, moved into the "Piney Woods" area of east Texas. By the time they became known to history there were more than two dozen tribes forming three confederacies up into modern day Oklahoma and west to the Trinity river. Though all these tribes had different names they all spoke Caddo. With their well-developed agricultural skills, their temple mounds with a dominant priestly class and an equally well-developed political system, the Caddo were the most advanced, productive and populous people of the land. The Caddo also practiced the custom, seen in the Maya and other South American people, of binding the head of newborns so that the skull became elongated, tapering to the top. Mayan rulers accentuated the effect by wearing a rubber artificial nose that tapered down from their forehead. While predominantly agriculturalists, growing different kinds of corn, squash, sunflowers, tobacco and five or six varieties of beans, they also hunted deer and bear with the aid of their dogs, which they also ate in lean times. They produced a lustrous black leather by tanning deer hides with deer and buffalo brains. Birds, rabbits and other mammals, snakes and fish filled out their diet together with wild fruits and nuts. They fished mostly with trotlines, a method they introduced to European settlers.

Given their location, it was inevitable that they would be some of the first indigenous to encounter Europeans. The Spanish and the French. The Spanish first, in 1541 a few unfriendly bouts of rape and pillage were followed by a period of no contact that lasted about 150 years. Then the Spanish were back and then the French. Once the Spanish learned that the French were invading what they considered to be "their land," expeditionary forces with priests were sent to establish colonies and missions. Fighting went on between the two countries, each recruiting different tribes, each trying to grab control. In 1762 France ceded Louisiana to Spain, though it later returned to France for a brief time. In 1821 Texas became part of an independent Mexico, then a Republic, during which its second President, Mirabeau Lamar, unlike its first, Sam Houston, who had been adopted into the Cherokee tribe and pressed for Native American rights, decided that Indians should leave or be killed. Throughout those trying times the Caddo, like the other Indian tribes, suffered the loss of their traditions and cultural ways. In 1835 the Caddo were forced to cede all their land, about a million acres, to the Government of the USA. In 1846 Texas became the 28th State of the USA. In 1859 the Caddo were force marched to Oklahoma joining another Texas tribe, the Tonkawa and others in "Indian Territory." The Caddo Nation of Oklahoma is a federally recognized tribe based in Binger, OK where the Caddo Heritage Museum, the Kiwat Hasinai Foundation and the Education Department strive to nurture the economic, social, religious and cultural heritage of the Caddo.

Cool Fact: The tribes of the Caddo confederation called each other, *Tayshas,* "friends" or "allies". The Spanish took up the word and the pronunciation went from *Tayshas* to *Taychas* to *Tejas*, Texas.

What other Tribal names start with C?

Diné

D is for Diné

Diné is what the Navajo called themselves, it means "The People" which is much the same way most indigenous people referred to themselves, everybody else, of course, not being "The People". The Spanish called them the Apaches of Navajo and the name Navajo stuck. The Navajo Nation territory of around 17,544,500 acres is in what is known as the Four Corners area where Arizona, New Mexico, Utah and Colorado meet. It is the largest Indian reservation in the USA and is larger than several states. How did that come about? Let's start back as far as we have any record.

It's generally accepted that the Navajo are related to the Athapaskan people of Alaska and Canada who began moving into the Southwest early on. Hunter/gatherers, the Navajo, like those before them, preyed on the Pueblo people, stealing what they could, enslaving their women and generally making their life miserable. Once the Spanish brought in sheep and goats the Navajo saw a way to settle down and be productive. The Pueblo women that were taken as wives, with their experience of weaving cotton, taught the Navajo women how to weave this new thing, wool. (It wasn't Spider Woman). By 1700 Navajo women were producing weavings that were, and still are, highly prized. The Navajo men had not given up their raiding ways which now included the Spanish the Mexican and the Anglo settlers. It was these last who in 1863 complained to the government. Kit Carson, famous as a trapper and guide, was commissioned as a Lt. Colonel in the Union army and tasked with the job of doing something about it. He led a brutal campaign that destroyed orchards, crops, entire Navajo villages and slaughtered their livestock. By 1864 he had captured most of the Navajo and marched them in what is known as the 'long walk' 300 miles to Bosque Redondo, a desert with little to no food or water where, predictably, many died. After four years it was obvious that it would be best if they went back to their ancestral land. Much hardship awaited them but the People persevered through land boundary disagreements, disputes with the BIA, the Bureau of Indian Affairs, and how they should govern their nation within a nation. Ever adaptable and persevering, the Navajo have survived overgrazing, they still deal with the adverse health effects caused by large scale uranium mining, now banned on their land, and coal mining, with its bad effects. Nearly half of the tribal members live off the reservation, many of those that remain live without electricity or running water in remote areas. This remoteness leads to under counting in census-taking and difficulty getting to vote when it comes to election time. Still, they are getting into wind-power and oil and gas leasing. Tourism and the casino business together with the never-ending demand for their weaving and their silver and turquoise jewelry, have arguably, made the Navajo the most successful and well adapted of all the tribes in the US. In Beauty May They Walk.

Cool Fact: During WWII Navajo servicemen in the US Marine Corps communications units seemed to be speaking in code to the enemy listening in. The almost unknown Navajo language with the additional use of word substitution made for an unbreakable code. Cherokee and Choctaw speakers pioneered this kind of 'code' talking in WW1.

What other Tribal names start with D?

Eskimo

E is for Eskimo

Eskimo is another of those names that came about due to either a misunderstanding, a mispronunciation or mistranslation. Eskimo has been translated as "snowshoe netter" "to net snowshoes" or "a person who laces snowshoes". Another translator thought it meant "people who speak a different language". Nothing offensive about that, right? Still others derive it from a word that meant "eats something raw" Eskimos then being "eaters of raw meat". If you ever dined at a Japanese sushi restaurant you wouldn't find anything offensive in that, however, it has become considered a put-down and the Canadian Government has replaced Eskimo with Inuit. Alaska still has Eskimo and the choice is yours. There are numerous languages and dialects among the native people of Alaska, Canada and Greenland who fall under the grab-bag of Eskimo or Inuit. When you consider the thousands of years people have occupied the area, having migrated there from Siberia speaking different languages, it's not surprising that many are unintelligible to their neighbors and some that have died out completely. In order to survive the extremely harsh polar conditions the Eskimo developed some unique tools. The names for which have become part of the English language. *Kayak,* the skin covered canoe that is basically worn by the kayaker, his skin jacket attaches to the boat creating a watertight vessel from which to fish and hunt. In the event the kayak overturns it can be righted without taking on water. They developed the Harpoon with a detachable tip that had a long line attached, a bladder float made from a bird's gullet that kept the spear part afloat after a seal, whale or narwhal had been struck. They also developed their own throwing-stick, similar to the Atlatl. One ounce of narwhal skin contains as much vitamin C as one ounce of orange juice. Without fruit or vegetables this was a vital commodity just as the contents of the stomach of a grazing animal such as the reindeer or caribou was a special healthy treat. The Inuit are still allowed a subsistence hunt. They wore a bird skin shirt with the feathers turned in, edged with dog skin over which they wore an *Anorak* of sealskin, sealskin trousers, sealskin shoes of two layers, the first had the fur inward, the second with the shaved skin facing out. Men and women dressed the same though the women added color where they could. Mothers wore an *Amaut* of reindeer skin that had a large pouch to carry their baby in. Inside their stone or snow houses, the *Igloo*, heated with oil lamps, which they kept burning day and night, both sexes wore virtually nothing. In the summer months when most of their hunting was done, small skin tents were used as shelter. Small sculptures made of a variety of stone, whalebone, Caribou bone and antler along with Walrus ivory and Narwhal tusk became popular trading items and remain popular art objects today. Baleen, the filter that hangs from the top of a whale's mouth was cut into thin strips for basket-making and for use in jewelry.

The Inuit of Labrador were the first to encounter Europeans, the Vikings, for a short period then about a century later, Basque Whalers. Encounters with French and English trappers were generally peaceful but, as with other indigenous people, infectious diseases for which they had no immunity, resulted in mass die-offs. Mistreatment and neglect on the part of those governments that came to control the Eskimos lands transformed these self-sufficient hunters into helpless wards. But they survived and their situation has improved. Nowadays, snowmobiles have mostly replaced dogsleds and rifles the harpoon. Furs and skins are still the preferred dress against the cold. While many have totally abandoned the old ways except for observing the traditional dances and handicrafts, the Eskimo remain a distinct and proud people.

Cool Fact: C. K. Nelson (1893-1992) produced a chocolate covered ice cream in Onowa, Iowa and sold it under the name, "I-Scream Bars". He joined up with Russell Stover to mass-produce them under the name "Eskimo Pie". By 1922 they were selling one million a day.

What other Tribal names start with E?

Flathead

F is for Flathead

Flathead was the name Europeans gave to the Salish and Kootenai people. The Flathead reservation where the Bitterroot Salish, Kootenai and Pend d'Orielles tribes live is in Montana. The Salish having moved there from the West Coast, and the Kootenai and Pend d'Oreilles from Idaho, Canada and parts of Montana. The reservation occupies a fraction of their traditional lands, it was created in 1855, in 1904 the federal government allotted either 80 or 160 acres to tribal members, the rest was opened to white settlers; for logging, schools and missionaries. At one point the commissioner of Indian Affairs made deals with a power company to use Flathead land without even bothering to let the tribe know. Naturally, the natives weren't too happy about these kinds of arrangement and some deadly clashes took place in the process. Today the Flathead own only about two thirds of the reservation land; they continue to buy back what they can as they have done for many years. Kootenai National Forest and Flathead National Forest border the reservation, the Blackfoot reservation is to the east and other tribal lands are nearby. That part of Montana has been occupied for more than 14,000 years by hunter/gathers. The abundance of wildlife which still includes bison was a big draw while the 197 square mile Flathead Lake provided a plethora of fish. Most of the lake is within reservation land, Flathead State Park is on the northern shore. Recently, the annual fishing tournament catch was 402,000 lake trout. Keeping State, Federal and Tribal rules and regulations straight is often a problem. Cherry orchards and vineyards grow along the shores; shoreline real estate is highly valued. To all of these attractions add the reservation's resort and casino that cater to visitors. Once illegal, the six-day Powwow held on the 4th of July week features traditional songs and dances. Timber, the electric power plant dam, plus the manufacture of electrical components, makes the Flathead some of the better provided native peoples. In the 1800's Captain Bonneville, who pushed for spreading the fur trade to some of the wilder tribes, said this; *"Simply to call these people religious, would convey but a faint idea of the deep hue of piety and devotion which pervades the whole of their conduct. Their honesty is immaculate; and their purity of purpose, and their observance of the rites of their religion, are most uniform and remarkable. They are, certainly, more like a nation of saints than a horde of savages."*

Pend d'Oreilles? Translates as, "Ear loops" or "hangs from ears". That is what the French *voyageurs* called the people they encountered. It was for the large shell or bone earrings they wore. Kootenai also came from the French. The Pend d'Oreilles were also known as the Kalispel which translates as "Camas People." *Camissia* roots, of the *Camasia* genus. Camas roots were an important part of many tribes' diets, pit-roasted, boiled or ground into flour once they were dry. The Camas prairies were greatly diminished when settlers released their cattle and hogs on the land. Not to be mistaken for the white flowering Death Camas, *Zigadensis* genus.

Cool Fact: The name Flathead was given to the members of the Salish who *did not* practice cranial deformation. The Salish used a method to make their heads rounder so, the Flatheads were the ones with normal heads. The practice of deforming the skull dates back thousands of years and was carried out around the world. It is still practiced today in a few areas. The effect most commonly seen was the result of strapping a board attached to a mother's carrying cradle that pressed down on the forehead of the child. A variety of similar methods were carried out to obtain the distinctive appearance that was considered an important feature of their identity, rooted in some aspect of their past and perhaps, their concept of beauty. The cradle board allowed the mother to carry out her daily chores which included foraging for food in the form of nuts, fruits, bulbs, seeds etc. not to mention all of the other tasks that were the province of women.

What other Tribal names start with F?

GOSHUTE, GOSHIUTE OR GOSIUTE

G is for Goshute, Goshiute or Gosiute

The Goshute, a spelling that has many variants, referred to themselves as *Newi* "person" or "People" just as we have seen with other people but additionally, *Gutsipiute* "People of the Desert" a most appropriate name as we shall see. As part of the Western Shoshone who occupied what is now southeastern California through central and eastern Nevada, northwestern Utah into parts of Idaho and Wyoming they spread throughout the Great Basin as hunter/gathers in small family groups gathering with other family groups in simple villages in winter and for short communal hunts lasting no more than 2-6 weeks. Communal hunts were for large game such as elk, deer, bear, pronghorn and bighorn sheep as well as coyote. They ate small mammals from gophers and rabbits to skunks and squirrels. Women and children gathered nearly one hundred species of plants for roots, flowers, seeds and nuts. Insects such as red ants, grasshoppers and crickets were included while fish, lizards, snakes and birds made up the rest of their diet. This hard but idyllic life was not to last. Unlike their relatives, the Comanche and other tribes, they avoided the horse when it came along seeing it would trample the delicate grasslands upon which they depended. The Spanish, who brought the horse, came to carry them off as slaves. Then Mormons settled in Salt Lake Valley and soon began to invade Goshute territory, their cattle overgrazed the meadowlands the Goshute had tried to preserve. Since the Mormons believed that God had given them this Promised Land, Goshute claims meant nothing to them. The Goshute confiscated cattle and horses they found on their land which, predictably, set off conflict. Mormon militias killed some Goshute together with their allies the Timpanogos, continuing to push further into their lands. Soon Goshute land became a regular highway as wagon trains of emigrants to California, the Pony Express, the Butterfield stage-coach service and telegraph lines followed the route as military camps were setup. Now Mormon ranchers and farmers moved in taking the best land and water resources. The land that had sustained them for thousands of years could no longer meet the demand. In the early 1860's the Federal army attacked and forced those they did not kill into signing a treaty which, although they were not required to give up sovereignty of the land, gave permission for all that had gone before and more of the same, plus, railways, mining, timber cutting and timber mills. Things only got worse in the twentieth century. The Skull Valley Indian Reservation, covering 28.187 sq. miles is inhabited by the Skull Valley Band of Goshute Indians of Utah, a federally recognized tribe. It is surrounded by a hazardous waste landfill, a nerve gas storage facility, two hazardous waste incinerators; chlorine gas is released from one plant while another gives off toxic chemicals. A deal to store nuclear waste on the reservation didn't go through but the US Army tests the VX nerve agent at a facility around the reservation. This extremely toxic agent, in an incident, for which the Army never admitted fault, killed 6000 sheep belonging to the Goshute. The area where this occurred remains a hazardous waste site. What does the twenty first century hold for the Goshute? The Goshute are survivors, this they have proved through the centuries. They will continue to hold to their beliefs and their vision that have sustained them against all odds. Firm in their ways, they will prosper. They always have.

Cool Fact: For thousands of years indigenous people etched images in the rock at what is now the Parowan Gap petroglyphs State Park in southern Utah. For the people that made them, these enigmatic signs held both religious and calendrical significance. They certainly weren't the equivalent of "Kilroy was here".

What other Tribal names start with G?

HOPI

Michael Lawry

H is for Hopi

Hopi land is completely surrounded by Navajo land. It's a long story, full of the usual disputes over where one ends and the other begins, whose rights are being violated, who's trespassing, who gets to decide, etc., etc. Centuries have gone by with a settlement of sorts being arrived at only in 1992 when the Hopi reservation was increased to 1.500,000 acres. With no solid boundary, Hopi corn fields will always be a temptation to Navajo sheep and goat flocks. The villages of Oraibi, Shongopovi, Mishongnovi and Walpi each on their own mesa make up the pueblo. The Hopi are known as "The Peaceful People." The Hopi dictionary gives the primary meaning of Hopi as, *"One who is mannered, civilized, peaceable, polite, who adheres to the Hopi Way, in contrast to warring tribes that subsist on plunder."* This concept was put to the test when the Spanish arrived. First contact with the Spanish was in 1540 but it wasn't until 1629 that Franciscan friars came to build a church. As one of the more important villages of the Hopi, Awatovi was chosen as the site. Imposing the inquisition, they punished those who continued to adhere to Hopi religion; they were not too successful in converting many tribal members. The Hopi joined in the Pueblo Revolt of 1680 targeting the Awatovi soldiers, friars and priests who were killed, their church and mission buildings dismantled. Some twenty years later missionaries tried again but after a Franciscan Missionary converted a number of people there in 1700, religious leaders in the other villages, fearing the Hopi traditions might be threatened, decided to solve the problem by killing everyone they could, removing women and children and, stone by stone, totally destroying the entire village of Awatovi. The Spanish never went back. In 1847 the Mormons tried, then in 1887 a federal boarding school was setup to teach Hopi youth the ways of the white man. There they were made to give up their traditional names, ways, language and dress. Boys had their long hair cut, girls were taught modern household chores. All students were made to attend Baptist service every morning. Oraibi parents refused to send their children and were threatened with arrest. The director of the BIA, the Bureau of Indian Affairs, forcibly took children for the school 35 miles away. When a day school was built in Oraibi traditionalists still refused to let their children attend. 19 parents were arrested by government troops and sent to Alcatraz Penitentiary for a year. Finally, someone in a position to do something about it, got the Indian Reorganization Act of 1934 passed. It did away with the attempt at assimilation and encouraged the continuation of tribal traditions and culture. The Hopi ratified a constitution in 1936 and are now governed by an elected Tribal Council. While continuing to observe their traditional religion, clan organization and yearly cycle of ceremonies that take place according to the lunar calendar, they are also a part of the US economy with oil and coal leasing, hotels, restaurants, museums and gift shops where Hopi blue corn can be found together with the arts and crafts of Hopi artists, some of whom are justifiably famous. In the spring, ceremonies performed by dancers dressed as kachinas, the supernatural beings that connect the world of the living to the world of the spirit, are carried out as a form of prayer that, it is hoped, will bring the rain that gives life to the desert and the crops the Hopi depend upon. Kachina dolls were given to children that they might learn about the Hopi spirit world. They have become the most familiar and highly valued works of art the Hopi produce.

Cool Fact: Hopi two-time Olympic distance runner and silver medal winner in 1912, Lewis Tewanima, was a teammate of Jim Thorpe. Every year a race dedicated to him is held on Second Mesa. It begins on the top of the Mesa, follows a trail down and around the Mesa and ends with a climb up stairs back to the top for the finish line.

What other Tribal names starts with H?

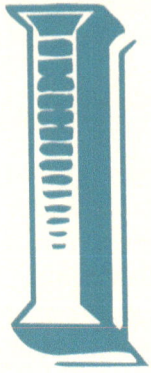

IIPAI

I is for Iipai

Iipai, Tipai-Ipai, meaning Man, or People, Kumeyaay-Kamia these are all names of the people who occupied what is now southern California and northern Mexico for some 12,000yrs. Stone scrapers and choppers indicate that other people had lived along the part of the coast they now occupy 20,000yrs ago. As hunter/gatherers they moved up into the mountains in the summer and back to the coast in the winter. Utilizing high altitude, desert and coastal plants and wildlife. They gathered acorns from a variety of oak trees which they learned to process so as to remove the tannic acid, also pine nuts and a wide variety of roots, fruits and any number of foods nature had to offer. They used the salicin found in willow as an insect repellent. Willows also provided the frames for their huts that were covered with a tule thatch. Their villages would consist of hundreds of these huts housing one family each. They were by no means a consolidated tribe, hence the various names. A variety of languages and dialects were spoken and often, as elsewhere, was incomprehensible to their neighbor. Their mythology was shared with neighboring tribes and their Shamanism was similar. Dances, song cycles and ceremonial ground paintings were carried out at specific times of the year.

Although information traveling along the trade routes from further south had already alerted them that strange white men had arrived from abroad, it wasn't until 1547 that a Spanish ship appeared in the bay beside which they spent their winters. In 1769 soldiers, explorers and missionaries came to settle in the Kumayaay village that occupied what is now Old Town, San Diego and the People became known as, Diegueños. The native population in 1776 was estimated at 150,000. As we have seen elsewhere, the heavy-handed attempts to "civilize" the natives did not go well. The mission established by the Spanish was burned down by the Iipai in 1775. The mission was rebuilt and in 1779 it had 1,405 neophytes. Still, at that same time, Lt. Colonel Pedro Fages noted; *"Indeed this tribe, which among those discovered is the most numerous, is also the most restless, stubborn, haughty, warlike and hostile toward us, absolutely opposed to all rational subjection and full of the spirit of independence."* After Mexico obtained its independence from Spain it secularized the missions, the secular administrators treated the natives like serfs, they became trespassers on their ancestral lands. Mexico made large land grants in order to attract settlers and a few Mission Indians managed to obtain some. Settlers were able to occupy whatever land they wanted. When the USA took over, the US senate rejected a treaty that had been made with "the nation of Dieguiño Indians." Efforts to obtain legal title to what lands they did own were unsuccessful. White squatters moved in as California boomed with the Gold Rush. The Tipai-Iipai reservations established in 1875 were inadequate for their traditional way of life. Those that didn't gravitate to the San Diego slums moved up into the mountains where, for a while they were able to continue their old ways. Acculturation slowly took its affect and people adapted to modern ways. While more natives live off the reservation than on, it remains the focal point of their culture and the center for all tribal activities.

To learn more about the Tipai- Iipai, Kumeyaay and how they live today, visit their various websites particularly; Kumeyaay.com

Cool Fact: A dance the Iipai performed when the piñon nuts were harvested in the fall, was called the Piñon Bird Dance, it was named for the Jays that competed noisily for the nuts. It is still performed today along with many other traditional dances.

What other Tribal names start with I?

J JICARILLA

J is for Jicarilla

J is for **Jicarilla**

The Jicarilla Apache Nation Reservation occupies a small part of what was once the Jicarilla's traditional hunting grounds. It straddles the borders of New Mexico and Navajoland, its Southwest corner borders Colorado; the Southern Ute Reservation is close by. The Jicarilla called themselves, *Haisndayn* "People who came from below" considering themselves to be the sole descendants of the first people to emerge from the underworld. Variations on this belief is found among a variety of peoples throughout the Americas.* The migration of Athapascan speaking hunter/gatherers from the western subarctic region occurred over a long period of time with people in that language group being found as far south as northern Mexico evolving culturally as they interacted with the residents they often displaced or assimilated with. We see this with the Navajo and the Hopi. The Jicarilla were closest with the Taos Pueblo natives. Archaeologists and anthropologists have long studied these people to determine how such a relatively small group came to dominate so many parts of the continent. The six Apache tribes gained a reputation as fierce warriors, the Mescalero and Chiricahua, with their leaders, Geronimo and Cochise in particular, were responsible for that, while the Jicarilla appear to have done little or nothing to change the culture of those with whom they assimilated or to change the new landscape into which they moved. Their approach was plant a little, hunt a little, and gather a little, always as the times were right as indicated by nature. The Jicarilla largely ignored the Spanish when they came. Still, they could not avoid the turmoil and disruption their arrival brought about. Just as we have seen elsewhere, resistance was met with aggression which was met with more resistance. Things did not improve once the white settlers moved in and the US military took over. A statement by Lt. Colonel John R. Baylor might sum it up; he called for the extermination of all adult Apache and selling their children, "to defray the cost of killing the Indians." From an estimated population of 10,000, by 1897 the Jicarilla had fallen to 300. Disease, war and famine had taken their toll. The Jicarilla reservation had been established in 1887 giving them citizenship and the right to own land which until then had been denied. The Jicarilla Nation now has more than 3000 members; it has a strong economy based on oil and gas leasing, sheep-herding and casinos. Visitors can avail themselves of the highly regarded basketry for which they are justly famous and other arts and craft works.

*Note; The sacred clown is an important participant in all ceremonies and celebrations bringing not just hilarity but also insights. Pueblo clowns led their people out of the earth (ignorance) into the sunlight (knowledge). The Jicarilla Apache did not see this world as purely good, the holy clown that led them out of the underworld was equipped with a "horrible non-human laugh" designed to scare away the sickness on the earth's surface. During ceremonies the clowns make people laugh but scare them too. This way, any worries or self-destructive thoughts they might have, are shocked out of them.

President George Washington 1732-1799 1st president of the USA was not the first to hold the opinion that any treaty or pact with the indigenous people was, *"A temporary expedient to quiet the minds of the Indians."*

Cool Fact: Jicarilla, (He-ka-ree-ya) Spanish for little basket, was bestowed upon them for the small sealed basketry drinking vessels that they carried with them when away from home.

What other Tribal names start with J?

Kiowa

K is for Kiowa

The Kiowa were a nomadic, Tanoan speaking people, a language they shared with the Pueblo people of New Mexico. That's one oddity. Their place of origin is unknown. Their lore claims they were called into existence in an area close to the headwaters of the Missouri and Yellowstone rivers in what is now Montana. Unlike so many tribes whose name came down to us either from what another tribe or the French called them or from a misunderstanding of what a tribal member replied when asked, the Kiowa called themselves the Kiowa. To the Kiowa this meant, "Principal People" however, linguists have trouble coming to agreement on its actual meaning. At some point in the 1600's the Kiowa moved to the Black Hills of Dakota, there they formed an alliance with the Crow Indians and had stable peace and trade relationships with surrounding tribes. Conflict with the Comanche on their southern hunting grounds developed into full-scale war around 1770 and peace with the other surrounding tribes ended. In 1781 while fending off threats from all directions, smallpox killed some 2000 Kiowa leaving just 300 warriors. In 1785 two-thirds of the tribe migrated to the Southern plains. Those that remained fought on but in 1795, on the brink of starvation, they left to join the rest of the tribe. In New Mexico the Kiowa formed an alliance with their arch-enemy the Comanche. This unlikely alliance was brought about, like so many others, by the transcontinental movement of natives displaced by Spanish, French and other European settlers which continued for the rest of the century. One tribe allied with the government against other tribes then would ally with other tribes against the government. No alliance could be depended upon to last. Attempts by the US government to forge a peace treaty between the warring tribes and the US was not too successful. Although a treaty between the Kiowa and the government was signed in 1837 one Kiowa chief refused to sign the document and the fight for survival continued. The influx of Euro-American settlers brought cholera on top of the smallpox. The tragic story we have seen unfold elsewhere inexorably became that of the Kiowa. With the bison gone, much of their traditional lands gone, the 20th century offered little and the federal government took away what little remained. Eleven years of litigation did produce a victory in 1960 when the tribe was awarded nearly $2million. By that time the tribe was dispersed, some living in California while some remained on scattered parcels of former reservation lands in Oklahoma. The Kiowa tribe of Oklahoma is federally recognized with its headquarters in Garnegie, Oklahoma where efforts to preserve Kiowa culture with traditional dances and the teaching of the Kiowa language together with traditional arts and crafts, serve to remind us all that the Kiowa are not going away.

Cool Fact: A sage Native American felt that since Christopher Columbus thought he had arrived in India when he got to the Americas, he should be forgiven for calling the natives, "Indians." He was grateful that Columbus hadn't believed that he had arrived in Turkey.

This is our country.
We have always lived in it.
We always had plenty to eat because the land was full of buffalo.
We were happy….Then you came….We have to protect ourselves.
We have to save our country. We have to fight for what is ours.
White Bear, Kiowa Chief
What other Tribal names starts with K?

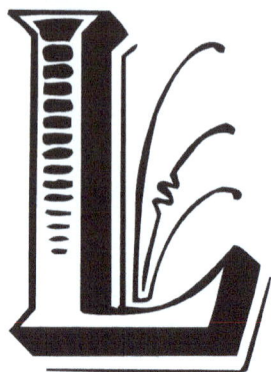

LUMMI

L is for Lummi

The Lummi or, Lhaq'temish (Lock-tuh-mish), "The People of the Sea" are well named. For 12,000yrs they have lived along the coast of Washington State, San Juan and Lummi islands and up into Canada fishing the sea. The forests along the coast provided fruits and vegetables and game. Most importantly, the cedar trees provided the wood from which they constructed their multi-family Longhouses and canoes as well as material for ropes and basketry. Fishing was and remains what they are about. Salmon, of which there are five different species, has always been their most important catch but there are 200 other species of fish, 200 kinds of sea birds, 26 species of sea mammals, shellfish and plants that provide a well-rounded diet. Seasonally, in harmony with the annual salmon runs, the Lummi moved from the mountains to the sea. With stone tools they felled the huge cedar trees, hollowed them out to make ocean-going vessels that allowed them to fish in Puget sound with their "reef nets" a method that has been recognized as the best for selective fishing. This life style began to change somewhat with the coming of European settlers in the early 19th century. With the Port Elliott Treaty of 1855 The Lummi, together with other tribes in Washington State, sold their ancestral lands and moved to reservations. One feature of the treaty proved to be of great value, it acknowledged the right of the people to continue to fish the waters their ancestors fished. Not only did this concession give access to large fishing grounds; the usual Nation within a Nation questions of when do States regulations apply and when do they conflict with the rights of Indigenous people still constantly arise, but it had a huge environmental impact. The proposed Gateway Pacific Terminal for the export of coal was fiercely fought by the Lummi and equally fiercely supported by labor unions and those looking for employment. The battle continued for many years but in 2016 the Army Corps. of Engineers denied the permit citing the Lummi Nation's treaty-protected fishing rights, although there were many other environmental concerns that played a part. Terminal proposals have not gone away and the struggle to protect the environment of the Pacific coast area continues. Overfishing due to the increase in commercial and individual fishing is one of the challenges the Lummi face as salmon catches decline. Population growth, degraded watersheds, agricultural fertilizer and pesticide runoff are being confronted by the Lummi working in concert with inter-tribal, government and scientific groups to secure a sustainable future. The LNR, Lummi Natural Resource Department, monitors the reservation beaches for "red tide" and other toxins in the water that could make shellfish and other fish unsafe to eat. The Tribal Canoe Journey in which many of the Indigenous people of Alaska, British Columbia and the State of Washington participate has been revived and in 2007 the Lummi hosted their first Potlatch since the 1930's. The Potlatch in which material possessions are given away, was an important feature of life among the people of the Pacific Northwest. Those with little were helped out and those that gave obtained prestige. The more one gave away the higher the prestige and the higher one's non-material possessions. The Federal government banned the Potlatch in 1884 seeing it as anti-Christian, reckless and wasteful of personal property. At times it did get out of hand when valuable items were deliberately destroyed, but it was secretly continued as a celebration to give to others.

Cool Fact: Chief Seattle who signed the Port Elliott treaty, sided with the settlers during the Indian uprisings of 1855-58. Grateful residents decided to name their growing town Seattle in his honor. Seattle objected on the grounds that his eternal sleep would be disturbed whenever mortals spoke his name. A small tax on the settlers as advance compensation for the disturbance settled the problem.

What other Tribal names start with L?

MANDAN

M is for Mandan

The Mandan called themselves, See-pohs-kah-nu-mah-kah-kee, "People of the Pheasants." Perhaps one of the most ancient tribes of the USA, their origins are lost in mystery and obscurity, they insisted that they were the first people created on earth. They occupied two villages on the west bank of the Missouri river about two thousand miles above what is now St. Louis and 200 miles below the mouth of the Yellowstone river. The villages were situated on the high bank of the river which formed a right angle at that place. On the other two sides were a fence and a ditch further protecting them from attack. In 1832 the painter, George Catlin stopped there on his canoe trip down the Missouri and spent some time painting portraits and scenes of village life. Warriors in all their finery were Catlin's main subjects, when he proposed to paint some of the dandified men who hung around his cabin, Chiefs he had painted told him he could not. They were homosexuals. Catlin described the people, their homes and burial grounds along with many other aspects of their lives in his notebooks a read I highly recommend. Their closely spaced, domed circular homes were very spacious, capable of holding 20-40 people and solid enough that entire families could lounge on the roof. Catlin described the interiors as clean and very attractive with screened beds each with its own post upon which were hung a vivid display of furs, trinkets and the armaments of the owner. Although always in some kind of conflict with the Sioux, village life was full of games, celebrations and dances, some being of deep religious consequence but others simply for pleasure. Their favorite was a game not seen among other tribes: on a smooth, hard clay pavement, a stone ring about three inches in diameter was bowled along followed by two players from different teams, each with a stick. The sticks were some six feet in length and had short bits of leather projecting from their sides. Each player slid his stick along the ground with the aim that when the ring stopped and fell over it would fall on his stick and a piece of leather would protrude through the ring. Not easy, as you can imagine, but it grabbed the attention of all and large sums were gambled on the outcome, some staking everything they possessed, even their liberty.

The bison, as we see elsewhere, provided most of their food, clothing and tools. The men were either preparing to hunt, hunting or recounting their previous hunts; preparing for battle, fighting or recounting previous battles so, it was up to the women to carry out most of the daily work including a little agriculture, mostly corn. They also produced a durable, kiln fired pottery. Catlin noted that the ruins of nine other Mandan villages existed down river, abandoned due to war and disease. In 1837 a smallpox epidemic struck again leaving only an estimated 30 to 140 survivors, enemy tribes quickly took them as slaves. The last known full-blooded Mandan died in 1971 and there are only an estimated eight speakers of their language left today. The three affiliated tribes of Mandan, Hidatsa and Arikara (Sahnish) went through the same kinds of degrading government treatment as other native peoples which continues to this day. The reservation of nearly a million acres they were moved to, is in North Dakota. It sits on one of the largest oil and gas deposits in the USA.

Cool Fact: Being that there were blue-eyed and fair haired members of the tribe, rumors that a boat full of Welshmen had ventured up the Missouri at some time in the past, prompted a Welsh explorer to visit the Mandan in 1796. He later wrote: *Thus having explored and charted the Missurie (sic) for 1,800 miles and by my Communications with the Indians this side of the Pacific Ocean from 35 to 49 degrees of latitude, I am able to inform you there is no such people as the Welsh Indians.*

What other Tribal names start with M?

N

Narragansett

N is for Narragansett

The Narragansett are descendants of people who, according to archaeological and oral history, occupied Rhode Island more than 30,000 yrs. ago. By the time of the first documented contact in 1524, they were living in long houses that held up to twenty families in the winter, moving into Wigwams or Wetus in the summer. The Narragansett lived across the bay, named for them, from the Wampanoag who had lost a large number of their population to the epidemic of diseases brought by the English settlers. The Narragansett on the western side of the bay escaped the path of the diseases and having recently driven their enemy, the Wampanoag off the bay islands, seemed poised to take even more of the Wampanoag Confederacy territory. An English speaking member of the confederacy, who had been a slave in Spain, escaped to England, which is another story, happened to return to the area just before the *Mayflower* which you may have heard of, arrived. That was in December of 1620. Tisquanum, the escaped slave, was introduced to the Plymouth settlers and helped the Wampanoags make a peace treaty with them. An alliance they thought would help them in their fight with the Narragansett. The following fall when their harvest festival was held, the Pilgrims invited them to a holiday of Thanksgiving. A good time was had by all and they pledged to make it a regular holiday. Things went pretty well for the next 40yrs. but settlers continued to infiltrate their land, imposing laws that penalized the Wampanoags, trying to convert them from their traditional religion and tribal ways. Then came outright war, which spread to other parts of New England as more tribes took up the fight. The Narragansett, who had remained neutral, joined in after the English attacked one of their towns killing more than six hundred men, women and children. For a while it looked as though the natives might prevail but, aided by Indian mercenaries, the English won, executing the leaders and sending others into slavery in the Caribbean. Fifty five years after that thanksgiving feast only one hundred Narragansett and several hundred Wampanoag survived. Things only went downhill from there. The Narragansett lost their land then they lost the right to call themselves a tribe! The state of Rhode Island declared the Narragansett were no longer a tribe as its members were multiracial and pressured them to become US citizens. The Narragansett insisted they were a nation not a race. When testifying before the state legislature in 1876, this statement was made; **We are not negroes, we are the heirs of Ninagrit and of the great chiefs and warriors of the Narragansett. Because, when your ancestors stole the negro from Africa and brought him among us and made a slave of him, we extended the hand of friendship and permitted his blood to mingle with ours, are we to be called negroes? And be told that we may be made negro citizens? We claim that while one drop of Indian blood remains in our veins we are entitled to the rights and privileges guaranteed by your ancestors to ours by solemn treaty, which, without a breach of faith you cannot violate.**

The Legislature was unmoved. But, the people never lost hope nor did they lose their identity. The Narragansett Indian Tribe of Rhode Island finally regained federal recognition in 1983. The struggle for land continues. States rights, Federal laws, and Tribal rights continue to cause headaches but in 2017 the tribe held its 342nd Powwow with traditional celebrations and dances. The Narragansett language is being revived and tribal pride manifested.

Cool Fact: It was known that Algonquin tribes, (of which the Narragansett are members) cultivated maize, but there was no evidence of it until an archaeological dig carried out in 1987 on the island in Point Judith Pond, that had been pointed out to Roger Williams, the founder of the city of Providence, as the original home of the Narragansett, turned up 78 corn kernels, thus confirming for the first time that corn had been cultivated that far north on the Atlantic Coast.

What other Tribal names start with N?

OSAGE

O is for Osage

Osage, the French version of the Osages name for themselves translated as "calm waters" *Wa-saw-see,* what the Osage called themselves, translates as "mid-waters." How the French got 'osage' out of *Wa-saw-see,* I can't imagine. The tribe developed in the Ohio and Mississippi river-valleys around 700BCE so their name makes more sense. Unlike most other tribesmen the Osage warriors shaved their heads, not an easy process before Whites supplied steel knives, except for a two inch long tuft on the top of their head which was topped with a crest of red dyed deer tail or horse hair, and sometimes a war-eagle's quill. A lock of hair that was never cut, grew from the center of the tuft, carefully braided it was known as the *scalp-lock.* In the event the warrior was captured or killed this lock was his offering to the enemy in place of a full scalp. In addition these warriors painted their heads and most of their face red. Osage men were noted for being very tall, averaging 6 to 7 feet, they were also described as "The finest looking." Their children were subjected to the head-deforming cradle board but in this case the deformation was a flattening of the back of the head which, according to the Osage, gave a "more bold and manly appearance in front". While rejecting the luxuries and customs of the white man, including whiskey, the Osage, as with most every other tribe, suffered through the smallpox, the loss of their traditional hunting grounds, and Christianization. They were moved from their hunting grounds in Kansas to Indian Territory (Oklahoma). In the twentieth century oil was discovered on the land they had been forced to occupy. Leasing fees made many of the tribe wealthy. A good turn out for a change, right? Well, not really. A series of unsolved murders of Osage owners of oil royalties and even their heirs, from 1910 through the 1930's, estimated to be in the hundreds, went mostly uninvestigated. Although some men were convicted and sentenced, most of the cases were never pursued. The "Reign of Terror", as it became known, involved white opportunists bent on getting their hands on that money by any means possible. Marrying an Osage woman then killing her was a popular method. The Department of the Interior's appointing of 'Guardians' to eliminate the temptation to kill, led to even more corruption. At one time Pawhuska, the Osage County Seat, attracted 80 lawyers who helped guardians charged with criminal behavior to avoid punishment by settling out of court. In the twenty first century, after years of court action, the Federal government settled the mismanagement suit filed against the departments of the interior and treasury by the Osage for $380 million. Your tax dollars at work.

A number of fiction and non-fiction books, films, radio and television programs have been produced giving accounts of the Osage murders. *Mean Spirit* a first novel by Chickasaw author Linda Hogan on the subject, was nominated for the Pulitzer prize in fiction in 1991.

Thomas Jefferson, 1743-1826. 3rd president of the USA. When the Ohio and Illinois river valley Indians continued to resist white settlement, urged. *"their extermination or their removal beyond the lakes or Illinois river."*

Cool Fact: The Osage warriors hairstyle is best known as the Mohawk. The look was attained in a variety of ways including, plucking and the application of hot stones to burn the hair off. The practice of removing all the hair except for a 'top-knot' of some kind was seen among the Pawnee, Mohican, Mohegan and other tribes. It can be traced back to Mongolia and Khazakstan where mummies sporting mohawks have been found by archaeologists. 16th century Cossacks favored the look and a 2000yr. old mummy found in a bog in Ireland had a mohawk. The modern version seems to have caught on due to the influence of the film, *Drums along the Mohawk* that starred Henry Fonda.

What other Tribal name starts with O?

Paiute

P is for Paiute

There are the Northern Paiute, the Southern Paiute, the Mono, who broke down into the Eastern Mono and the western Mono bands, who intermarried with the Yokuts, it gets a little complicated. The Southern Paiute alone had 16 to 31 subgroups. All spoke what is known as, Uto-Aztecan languages. Over the course of time and the development of dialects, one band could have difficulty understanding another. Today, some dialects are dying out with very few remaining active speakers. Starting out as hunter/gathers they spread across the area now known as California, Nevada, Utah and into Oregon, settling along river valleys where they raised crops such as corn, melons and squash: members of the first John Wesley Powell expedition down the Colorado river in 1869, helped themselves to squash from Paiute gardens in the absence of the owners who, the expedition members assumed, were away hunting at the time. The subsequent expedition of 1871, lead again by Powell, was only successful thanks to the help of the Paiutes they befriended along the way. In California the Owens valley Paiute used irrigation to raise large stands of Indian rice grass among other plants. In Utah they welcomed the Mormons but there, as elsewhere, infectious diseases, to which they had no immunity, loss of land and the erosion of their traditions, took its toll. As curers, rainmakers, sorcerers and intermediaries with the spirit world, Shamans held a strong position in Paiute society as they did among most Native tribes. The Paiute shaman Wovoka is perhaps the best known. He was responsible for the Ghost Dance which, according to him, if carried out properly over the five days of its performance, would sweep away all evil, secure happiness, and bring about a renewed earth filled with food, love and faith. Wovoka's vision was based on his traditions and what he had learned of Christianity. The dance spread rapidly to other tribes. Ghost shirts, created for the dancers, were believed to have the power to repel bullets. The Lakotas that took up the dance, interpreted the idea of "all evil washed away" to include the removal of all the European Americans. Wovoka's teaching of peace and harmony deteriorated into the Wounded Knee Massacre and the Ghost Dance War resulting in the death of the Lakota spiritual leader Sitting Bull.

Today there are Paiute reservations throughout the western States, much of their traditional lands are now national parks or under water; Lake Powell on the Colorado provided for the growth of Phoenix, Denver and Los Angeles. It is sadly ironic that the lake named for him brought about the very thing that Powell had warned against, knowing that the arid landscape could not sustain large populations he advocated for settlement based on the land's natural hydrology. That didn't go down well with those pushing for "progress." Now, with the ever increasing demand for water, its waste and misuse together with the effects of climate change, we see water emergencies becoming increasingly alarming.

When Oregon became a state in 1859 it barred black people from living there. The streams of white settlers looking for a white utopia didn't realize that native Americans were in place already. There are nine federally recognized tribes including the Paiute, and several unrecognized tribes.

Benjamin Franklin 1706-1790 Founding Father. "*And, indeed, if it be the design of Providence to extirpate these savages in order to make way room for cultivators of the earth, it seems not improbable that rum may be the appointed means.*"

Cool Fact: The Paiute Deadfall Trap. Traps and snares were an essential part of the lives of native people long before recorded history. The Paiute Deadfall trap is a simple but extremely effective trap used for centuries; images of it can be found in Paleolithic artwork. It was revived in the 1970's by the US Fish and Wildlife Service for catching Coyotes.

What other Tribal names start with P?

QUILEUTE

Q Is for Quileute

The Quileute, like their neighboring tribes along the west coast of America, have been and continue to be influenced by and dependent upon the environment they occupy. Salmon and cedar provided for most of their needs. The seasonal migration of salmon determines the activities of all the people. Housing, clothing, transportation and a long list of articles come from the utilization of the cedar tree. Whaling was carried out in the large cedar canoes they made. Canoes still are used in tribal canoe races and the Quileutes participate in the annual Tribal Journey that brings tribes from Canada and the USA.

The Quileute were forced onto the reservation they now occupy on the Olympic peninsula in Washington State after signing a treaty in 1855. There is an oceanside resort and RV Park catering to tourists but the tribal school where Quileute culture and language are taught is right next to the ocean and a project is underway to move to higher ground where it will be safe in the event of a tsunami or an earthquake. The Quileute language belongs to the Chimakuan family of languages, the only other speakers, the Chimukum were virtually wiped out by Chief Seattle in the 1860's, they are now nearly extinct. Although the Quileute language is considered extinct, the few remaining tribal members who have some knowledge of the vocabulary are seeing to it that it is being taught in the tribal school. These elders are fully aware that the language of a people holds the key to the history and culture of that people. Take for instance the word Christmas, for Christians, it contains two thousand years of history, no enumeration is necessary, it's all there in that one word. The impact of contact with European colonizers followed the pattern of other tribes. Land loss. History and culture lose. The twist in the Quileute's story is that the resolution of a 50yr. Northern boundary dispute and their final recognition as a tribe by President Barack Obama, came about as the result of the huge popularity of a series of books, which became an equally popular series of films, the Stephanie Meyers, *Twilight Series*. Meyers' books, for better or wor*se*, were inspired by the Quileute origins myth. Similar to the myth of Adam and Eve, a supreme being, in this case, Qwati, the transformer, finding no people at the mouth of the Quileute river, took two wolves and turned them into people. These people became the Quileute. Wolves, whales and fish feature in the rituals and ceremonies that are an important part of tribal life. Meyers' fictional Quileute are able to transform into wolves, werewolves and vampires. From being virtually unknown, the tribe has become the destination for hordes of tourists looking for these shape-shifting Quileute. This has brought economic benefits to the area as *Twilight* oriented businesses cater to the fans. Predictably, some Quileute welcome the attention, while others are disturbed by the distortion of their cultural heritage or simply have no interest in the phenomenon.

William Tecumseh Sherman, 1820-1891 civil war General, said his troops would confront the Sioux *"even to their extermination, men, women, and children"* Ironically, Sherman's father gave him his middle name out of admiration for the Shawnee leader Tecumseh, 1768-1813.

Cool Fact: Close knowledge of nature was essential to the survival of all native peoples, the Abenaki of Vermont noticed that the branches of the Balsam Fir tree react to changes in the weather. They created the "weather stick" by taking a branch, still attached to a piece of the trunk and mounting it outside where it bends to point down in rain or snow and up when it's sunny. Weather sticks are still given to friends and family and can be bought as useful indicators of whether you might need your umbrella or your sun hat when you go out.

What other Tribal names start with Q?

Rappahannock

John Smith's Map of Virginia 1606

R is for Rappahanock

The Rappahanock is one of the eleven state recognized tribes of Virginia; they finally were given Federal recognition in 2018. How could it be, you might ask, that a people that have occupied a part of what is now Virginia for thousands of years had to wait that long to be acknowledged as a tribe. It's a long story. The Rappahanock River is 195 miles long emptying into the Chesapeake Bay. Villages of the Rappahanock were situated along the north shore and their hunting grounds were on the south side. There were more than 30 Algonquin speaking people in the area which was also a highway for peoples traveling north and south. During the Civil War the river served as a boundary of the eastern theater of the war. Tens of thousands of troops fought each other along its banks and some 10,000 black slaves escaped across to Union lines and freedom during the fighting. The Rappahanock River, its fertile valley and the bay had sustained the People for thousands of years, before English colonists 'discovered' the area. The Rappahanock met Captain John Smith in 1607 when he was brought to them to determine if he was the one who had murdered their chief and kidnapped some of the people; the perpetrator had been tall and Smith was short and fat so he was found innocent, (of those crimes, at least.) Illegal settlements started along the valley in the 1640's, in 1651 the Rappahanock sold the first piece of land to an English settler. It took over ten years of court battle to get payed, though not in full, just as other sales never were paid in full. The sticky question of who exactly owned the land is one that plagued every such transaction throughout the country. Certainly, there were no titles, deeds or anything to prove the land was that of those occupying it, or the one selling it. Respect for the land and the belief that they were bound to protect it as its stewards came from thousands of years doing just that. True, tribes fought over territory for access to the fruits thereof, whether animal or vegetable, but not over who owned it. Once this sank in, white settlers had no compunction about taking whatever they wanted. By the late 1660's, Frontier vigilantes and illegal settlement forced the Rappahanock to move away from the river on the north side, where they had always lived. Later they moved to the south side. The English vigilantes had decided that all Indians were their enemies and should all be killed. However, the Virginia Council set aside 3474 acres for the Rappahanock "about the town where they dwell" in 1682. One year later they were forcibly removed and relocated to Portabago Indian Town where they served as a human shield to protect white settlers from the New York Iroquois. In 1706 they were moved from Portabago by the Essex County Militia and their land was given to English settlers. The Rappahanock moved down river to their ancestral homeland where they reside today, working with the US army, that has a base there, to restore the land. They hold their traditional harvest festival and Powwow each year in October at their Cultural Center in Indian Neck, Virginia.

Cool Fact: The nation's first Immigration law was passed in 1790, it gave the right of naturalization to white immigrants. It took an Amendment to the constitution in 1868 to give birthright citizenship to blacks. Thirty years later the Supreme Court decided that persons of Asian descent also had birthright citizenship. It wasn't until 1924 that indigenous people born in the USA were declared to be citizens; however, those that were designated "wards of the State" did not obtain the right to vote until 1964. Even those tribes and tribal nations that theoretically have autonomy over their lands and lives are still greatly controlled by the BIA and other government agencies. This ambiguity about sovereignty is the reason tribal lands are constantly under threat of appropriation for such things as military bombing ranges or mining by private companies that receive approval from the federal government. Though technically not, "wards of the state", there's some question about that, most of the 2.6 million Native Americans, 21% of whom live on reservations, depend on government support in order to survive. Their poverty levels and unemployment levels are well above the nation's averages.

What other Tribal name starts with R?

Seminole

Michael Emry

S is for Seminole

"We ask and require you... to acknowledge the Church as the ruler and superior of the whole world, and the high priest called the Pope and in his name the King as lords of... this terra firma... (if you submit), we...shall receive you in love and charity, and shall leave you, your wives and children, and your lands, free without servitude.... But if you do not... we shall powerfully enter into your country, and shall make war against you... We shall take you, and your wives, and your children, and shall make slaves of them... and we shall take away your goods and shall do you all the harm and damage we can."

This was the *Requerimiento* that was supposed to be read to native peoples, in Spanish, of course, when conquistadors arrived in their lands. Since it usually wasn't translated, it really didn't mean very much. It's not known whether Juan Pónce de Leon delivered it when in 1513, he arrived on the Atlantic coast of the land he named, Pascua Florida, it being Easter, the time of the Feast of Flowers. Florida was home to numerous tribes, mostly living on shell mound complexes with extensive canal systems,* de Leon managed to kidnap a few before being driven off. He then went down around the Keys to the west coast, home of the most powerful, civilized and settled tribe in Florida, the Calusas. Their influence extended across Florida to the Atlantic and Lake Okeechobee, known to them as Mayaimi, (sound familiar?). He grabbed a few of these people before the Calusas fought him and his crew off. Years of invasion, fighting and broken treaties went by. In the 18th and 19th centuries what small groups of Calusas survived joined with Creeks and other immigrant bands from the north, becoming the Seminoles and Miccosukee nations of today. The Seminole soon came into conflict with slave owners of Georgia who claimed that blacks living with the Seminole were runaway slaves and they were out to recapture them. The Red Stick Creeks who made up a good part of the Seminoles, had fled to Florida in part to get away from Andrew Jackson and the US Army but, in 1818 Jackson marched his troops into Florida and attacked the Seminole, inconsequentially forcing the Spanish to cede Florida to the USA in 1819. In the 1830's war broke out again over the Seminoles resistance to moving to the prairies of Oklahoma. From 1835 to 1842, this effort cost the USA between 40 and 60 million dollars, the army lost 15 hundred soldiers and although more than 4000 Seminole were captured and sent to Oklahoma, where the majority live on the Seminole Tribe of Oklahoma reservation, it was considered the longest, costliest and least successful war against Native Americans in history. The Seminole have the distinction of being the only people never to have surrendered to the invader. There is no doubt that the swamps and dense forest of the Everglades played a big part in the government's decision to abandon the effort and leave the Seminole and their allies among the alligators, bears and panthers of their home. The Seminole Tit-Ka, the Ivory-billed Woodpecker to us, is considered, "most likely extinct" but the Seminole continue and thrive on their six Florida reservations, working in a number of different ways to maintain their independence.

*There are hundreds of shell mound complexes throughout Florida often with canal systems and causeways, some dating back 4 to 6000yrs., even older ones are said to lie off the coast, predating those of the *Woodland Era* mounds like Cahokia, Adena, Hopewell and many others across the country.

Cool Fact: It is contended that the Spanish evacuated the last of the Calusa to Cuba when Spain ceded West Florida to the Kingdom of Great Britain in 1763, (until 1783, when it was ceded back to Spain) suggesting that there were no Calusa left to become part of the Seminole. Seminole may derive from a Creek word, simanó-li, meaning "runaway" or "separatist". Alternatively, it has been said to derive from the Spanish, cimarrón, meaning "wild".

What other Tribal names starts with S?

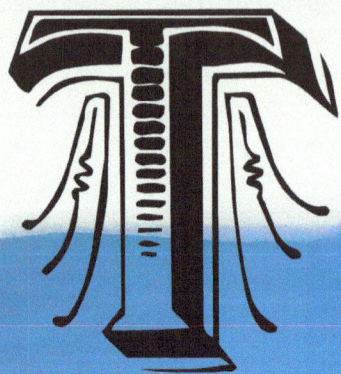

Taos

Michael Farny

T is for Taos

Taos Pueblo vies with Acoma Pueblo for the title of oldest continuously inhabited community in the USA. It is a UNESCO World Heritage Site and is on the US National Register of Historic Places. It is the most northern of the eight Northern Pueblos that follow the Rio Grande as it makes its way through New Mexico. The Taos and Picuris Puebloans speak Tiwa, the others speak Tewa, and both are closely related to the Tanoan family of languages spoken in NM, Kansas, Oklahoma and Texas. San Juan Pueblo, since 2005, known by its Tewa name of Ohkay Owingeh, serves as the Capital of the Eight Northern Pueblo Council. Taos Pueblo consists of 95,000 acres of tribal land with 4,500 members living in the area, only about 150 live within the historic complex. This multi-storied residential complex, built on either side of the Rio Pueblo, that runs from its source in the Sangre de Cristo Mountains thirty three miles to the Rio Grande, is believed to have been built between 1000 and 1450 CE. The Pueblo people are believed to be descendants of the Anasazi. Non-indigenous people are welcomed as day visitors; they can also attend some of the outdoor celebrations. A fee is charged for photographing. Taos in one of the most conservative Pueblos. Their language has never been written down, they are not in the habit of talking to outsiders about their religious customs and consequently, little is known about their culture. The Spanish came along in 1540, still looking for those Seven Cities of Gold. As elsewhere, Spanish Jesuits came and built a Catholic church around 1620 and as elsewhere, tensions arose with the resident priest being killed and the church destroyed. That didn't stop the Spanish rebuilding, which, among other things, led to the Pueblo revolt of 1680. What other things? Juan de Oñate put down a revolt at the Acoma Pueblo, angered that his brother had been killed in the fighting, he enslaved hundreds of people and cut off the right foot of all men the age of 25 and over. Puebloans were being used as slave labor to build the many missions and churches deemed necessary for their conversion, they were also forced to provide tribute in the form of food and textiles. Fray Alonso de Posada banned the Pueblos' Kachina dances and ordered the destruction of all religious objects not christian. Entheogenic drugs used in their religious ceremonies were forbidden. In 1675 Governor Juan Francisco Treviño ordered the arrest of 47 medicine men. Four were sentenced to death for "sorcery" all were publicly whipped and sentenced to prison. Pueblo leaders forced Treviño to release the prisoners, one of whom was Popé. Popé moved to Taos Pueblo and spent the next five years organizing a revolt. Not all the Pueblos joined in the revolt but enough did to expel the Spanish from New Mexico, pushing them across the Rio Grande at El Paso. The first attempt to return in 1681 was unsuccessful. Then in 1692 Diego de Vargas marched into Santa Fe unopposed, the Pueblos agreed to peace. However, de Vargas' harsh control set off another revolt which was put down unmercifully. The Spanish did see the light though and gave up their efforts to eradicate the Pueblos' culture and religion, they issued land grants and the Franciscans refrained from imposing their theocracy, opting for the long term conversion approach. There is a Catholic church within the walls of the residential complex.

Cool Fact: *Kino and Teresa*, an adaption of *Romeo and Juliet* written by Taos Pueblo playwright James Lujan, was performed in Los Angeles in 2005. The play is set five years after the reconquest of 1692, it links actual historical figures with their Shakespearean counterparts to show how different sides can learn to live together.

What other Tribal names start with T?

U

UTE

U Is for Ute

Utes had become a distinct Numic speaking people by 1000-1200CE in the area of what is now east California and south Nevada. By 1300 they had migrated to the Four Corners region by which time it is thought there was a 5000-10,000 population. It was at that time that the Paiute, Shoshone, Comanche and others separated off and went their own way. This left seven nomadic bands of Utes scattered over some 150.000 sq. miles of mountains and desert, land they were very proficient at utilizing and nurturing. As we have seen elsewhere, the tribes congregated at certain times of the year for celebrations; there was a Sun Dance and the Ute Bear Dance, carried out at the end of winter when bears, to whom they considered themselves related, came out of hibernation. The Ute acquired horses around 1640 or, perhaps as early as 1580, changing their way of life immensely. While remaining largely friendly to the Pueblos and the Spanish, they become feared warriors, harassing the Navajo to such an extent that they chose being moved to Bosque Redondo over remaining on their traditional lands. A move they soon regretted. Kit Carson had Ute mercenaries help move the Navajo. But pressures were starting to build on the Ute. The Spanish Colonial Government settled some 30,000 Hispanic mestizos in the area Utes considered theirs, making them easy pickings for the Ute raiders but stirring problems with the government. Brigham Young planned to establish his Mormon empire in Mexico but shortly after reaching Salt Lake City in 1877, it became the territory of Utah, in the United States. Still, his attitude toward the natives was; make friends, encourage the various tribes to make peace, convert them and then "civilize" them. That didn't work too well and in 1861 President Abraham Lincoln ordered the Basin Utes, who had come into armed conflict with Mormon settlers, moved from Provo valley to the Uintah valley creating the Uintah and Ouray reservation, 150miles east of Salt Lake City. What remained of their land was taken over by the government. Another treaty, in 1868, created the Colorado reservation for the other Ute tribes. Treaties and boundaries changed over the next few years. A clash over who was responsible for a fire in Wyoming resulted in all of the Utes in Wyoming being moved to reservations in Utah and Colorado. The Uintah Basin reservation is the second largest in the USA approximately 4.5 million acres with elevations from 5000 ft. to 13,000ft. The Green River runs through the reservation. There is an abundance of oil, gas, tar sands and oil shale on the reservation, Samuel H. Gilson, who was mining there illegally, discovered a material that, in all modesty, he named Gilsonite. 7,000 acres were removed from the reservation in 1888 so that mining could continue. Used in over 160 products Gilsonite was the main component of the japan black lacquer used on the Ford Model T. Forty seven Coal fired power plants in Turkey burn Gilsonite also known as Uintahnite, and Lignite, most of them exceed sulphur dioxide and carbon emission limits, emitting 1 kilogram of carbon dioxide for every kilowatt of electricity generated, over twice that of a gas-powered plant. From 5%-6% of energy is lost in transmission and distribution.

The Uintah and Quray has a population of around 3,000, half of whom live on the reservation. The Ute Fish & Wildlife Department manages 4 million acres of natural resources, conserving native species, endangered species and game species, including bison, while preserving habitat. Big game, waterfowl, upland game, fishing, camping and boating permits are available to non-tribal members. The Southern Ute reservation has a population of 13,000, the Mountain Ute reservation population is given as 2,000.

Cool Fact: One of the many plants used by the Ute, Bear Root *Ligusticum portieri* commonly known as Osha, grows throughout the Rocky Mountains at elevations over 7,000ft. It is antibacterial and antiviral and is used for colds and upper respiratory ailments. It can be drank as a tea or used topically in baths or compresses. It can also be made into ointment for indigestion, infections and arthritis. It was said to repel rattlesnakes when applied to the body.

What other Tribal names start with U?

Vision Quest

V is for Vision Quest

The Vision Quest, a term coined by anthropologists in the 19th century, applies to a number of different practices intended to assist initiates to attain awareness of the spirit realm. In its simplest form it consisted of a kind of "rite of passage"; around the age of 14-15yrs a youth may participate in a sweat lodge ceremony then would go off alone to fast and pray for as many days as it took to reach a state of being found through crying to the Great Spirit. This self-imposed sacrifice, deprivation and discipline moved the youth into a place where, his spirit creature would appear to him, in a dream or hallucination. This companion bird, animal, reptile or unknown being, will be his protector, given by the Great Spirit, for life. He will make his "medicine bag" at this time which will hold objects that he considers important to his spiritual well-being. This passage was never spoken of except in ceremonies or to a trusted member of his clan. The loss of ones "medicine" was perhaps the worst thing that could happen, if his medicine bag was lost in battle he must fight to repossess it or take one from an enemy he has killed. Only that way could his "medicine" be restored.

A man dressed only in a breach-cloth with a skewer run through each of his breasts, cords attached to the skewers reach to the top of a pole which bends under the weight of his body as he sinks back almost to the ground. Those drumming and singing encourage him to look at the sun. This continues all day until he is cut down. If he makes it through without fail, he will have earned his repute as a brave or mystery-man. Some tribes had other more torturous and bloody trials to which their young men were subjected in order that they have the aid, only the Great Spirit could give, for the hardships and pain that were an inevitable part of life. Those that aspired to be a shaman or medicine-man were subjected to similar trials to establish that they had been selected by the Great Spirit for the part. In some cultures apprentices began their spiritual training as young as 5yrs. of age. Medicine and spiritual guidance were considered as important to those cultures as it is to ours. Study and practice were important but fasting, sleep deprivation; self-immolation and the use of drugs were part of the training. It was not meant for everybody. Visions were considered sacred information given by the Creator and the ancients. Mind altering drugs were and continue to be an important part of peoples' search for answers to the mysteries of life. It maybe that they were discovered by accident, everything that grew would be considered a possible source of sustenance, trial and error was the only way to learn. Mind altering drugs have been used for millennia; there is good reason why they have been called, "the food of the gods". Those mind-altering drugs that "open the doors of perception" together with drumming, singing, fasting and the other disciplines required of the participants, were aids to finding the way. Tobacco was often used liberally to enhance the state of otherness. In the same way, burning frankincense, used in the Catholic church, is mildly euphoric and stimulating, it's classed as 'slightly hazardous' by the World Health Organization. The Peyote Way is the most widespread contemporary version of Christianity practiced by Native Americans. The introduction of Peyote from Mexico where it was and continues to be a vital part of Huichol and other tribes' religion was brought north possibly by the Mescalero Apache. Introduced to the Comanche and Kiowa it forms the basis of the Native American Church, one of several Native American/Christian religions that arose in response to colonization. An attempt to ban the use of peyote met with resistance and the ban was repealed, the Native American Church is allowed to use it legally in their worship. The desire to know something beyond the everyday of this world leads to the Vision Quest.

Cool Fact: South Texas is the only place In the USA where peyote grows, it is extremely slow growing, over-harvesting and poor harvesting methods has led to its being placed on the State's endangered species list. Grafting peyote to the San Pedro cactus produces a far more rapid growth. Just as St. Peter holds the keys to heaven, so the San Pedro cactus allows users, "to reach heaven on earth."

What Tribal names start with V

Wiyot

W is for Wiyot

The Wiyot people lived in permanent villages in the Humbolt Bay area of California for thousands of years. One of their villages was on Tuluwat Island. They greeted the first white newcomers to the area with a giant clambake. In 1851 their effort to coexist and assimilate was met with a policy laid out by the then Governor, in his State of the State address, he said, *That a war of extermination will continue to be waged between the races until the Indian race becomes extinct is to be expected.* The California Legislature passed bonds to finance local militias, Native Americans were killed by the hundreds, militiamen were compensated for their time and expenses. The writer, Bret Harte, was working in Union, across the Humboldt Bay from Eureka, as assistant editor of the Union *Northern Californian* in 1860 when a group of Thugs went to Tuluwat Island after the Wiyot men, who had been celebrating the first night of their two day annual World Renewal Ceremony, had left for supplies. With clubs, knives and hatchets the Thugs slaughtered every Wiyot they could find. Over the next five days they did the same in over a dozen other Wiyot villages. Harte, though he had never questioned the prevailing White bias, the paper's owner and editor was a proponent of "The only good Indian is a dead one" philosophy, was shocked that the very natives that were not causing problems for the settlers should be the ones attacked. He was sickened by the sight of old women and babies with their heads smashed in and wrote about the massacre. Locals were inclined to let it go, no investigation was launched. But, in part, due to Harte's coverage, the story reached San Francisco and soon was picked up by the *New York Times,* bringing unwanted attention to the town of Eureka. Harte saw that he was a marked man and left for San Francisco, never to return. His later fiction which was sympathetic to Native Americans, brought him fame. The Thugs, according to the investigating grand jury, could not be identified and so continued in their Indian-killing ways. The Wiyots? Those that survived were rounded up and moved to the Klamath River Reservation where the appalling conditions reduced their numbers even more. By 1910 only one hundred remained. Throughout the years, the Wiyots nurtured the memory of their homeland, in 2000 they bought the 1.5 acres site of their town on the island known as Indian island and are cleaning up the accumulation of contamination produced by its century long use as a shipyard. In 2014 the Wiyot returned to the island and in 2019 after 160yrs. Eureka City Council voted unanimously to return it to the Wiyot. Tuluwat Island is home again to the Wiyot who are bent on its complete environmental and cultural restoration.

President Andrew Jackson. 1767-1845 7th President of the USA was an aggressive promoter of the tribal removal policies. The elimination of the Five Civilized Tribes from the southeastern states during the 1830's topped his agenda.

Cool Fact: The EPA, the environmental protection agency, is collaborating with the Wiyot in the cleaning up of the ship repair facility as they are with any number of other tribes around the country whose land has been exploited by big corporations, Utility companies, businesses as well as government agencies. Your taxpayer dollars are going toward clearing up pollution such as; uranium, mercury, arsenic, sulphur contaminated water, pesticides, unspent munitions and other things the government doesn't want you to know about. The corporations responsible for the mess have no intention of cleaning it up. Together with the EPA many tribes have instituted recycling and composting services together with their cleanup efforts.

What other Tribal names start with W?

XL Ranch Band
of the Pit River Tribe

X is for XL Ranch Band of the Pit River Tribe

X. Often, in my other A to Z books I have resorted to making X stand for Extinct. Since I plan to deal with extinction in the bonus section, I was happy to find the XL Band. Not that the federally recognized nine bands of Achomawi and two Bands of Atsugewi all live on the XL ranch. The XL is the largest, at 9,255 acres, of several ranches or rancherias bought by the U.S. Government between 1915-1938 to house the Pit Rivers who were homeless by that time. The Alturas rancheria is the smallest, at 20 acres. All of the ranches are shared with members of other tribes. Like the other plots of land given to Native Americans under the 1897 General Allotment Act, the ranches are mostly unsuitable for farming. Consequently, most Pit River Indians don't live on Tribal lands. So, how did we get here? The Achomawi and Atsugewi once hunted deer by digging pits, into which the deer would fall, the river along which they lived became known as, Pit River and well, you get it. These People occupied part of northern California for 1000's of years as hunter/gathers using the natural resources and following the seasons. An abundance of Obsidian furnished them with material for tools and arrowheads, the bow and arrow were introduced to the area around 200CE. You should know that California has the most Native American tribes of any state in the Union, or second most, depending on your source, and at one time had even more. It was essentially full, not of individuals but of tribes and bands, when the first settlers came along. Those, of course, were the Spanish but, they didn't venture that far north. The XL's were spared that one but, in the 1820's European-American and Canadian fur trappers passed through the area. Sure enough, the natives started dying of imported diseases in the 1830's. White settlement increased bringing grazing animals that destroyed the natural environment, the settlers started appropriating land and fencing it off, dispossessing the native peoples. Wars and massacres got underway in earnest just as we have seen elsewhere. A Californio, as the Spanish settlers were known, was the first to find gold in 1842, prompting he and his fellow Californios to agitate for independence from Mexico. It was a find in northern California that set off the Gold Rush that started at the end of 1848, drawing the largest mass migration of people in American history. The word got out around the world and prospectors in their thousands started arriving in 1849, earning them the name, "Forty-niners." In all some 300,000 prospectors and those that wished to serve them or rid them of their treasure rushed in. The Gold Rush brought wealth to a few, most never made back the money it took to get them to California. It brought even greater hardship, starvation, loss of land and lives to the Native American population. Gold sped up the idea of admitting California to the Union and whether they knew it or not, the indigenous people became Californians when the state joined the Union in 1850. Not officially though, since the Pit Rivers never signed a treaty with the US government, the Congress and the California Legislature created laws that denied them land rights. The majority of the Pit River People were killed and their land seized. The US Army took over much of the upriver areas, (the Achoma/Pit River starts high in the mountains close to the border with Oregon and Nevada.) There, the government sold timberland for as little as $2.50 an acre. Much of the vast and diverse forests was over harvested bringing ecological problems that persist to this day.

The Pit River Tribe continue to hunt and gather in their traditional lands and pray at their sacred places. They own 79 acres in Burney, Ca. Where their headquarters are located. The Pit River Tribal Heritage Program THPO, provides educational outreach, public information and community seminars and promotes public awareness for the preservation and protection of cultural resources.

Cool Fact: The tribe operates a casino and has a large commercial cannabis growing facility which was raided by drug agents in 2015. In 2016 The Adult Use of Marijuana act was passed in California. Marijuana could become a bigger source of income for the Pit Rivers than gambling. Don't Bogart that joint, my friend.

What other Tribal names start with X?

Yaqui

MICHAEL EARNEY

Y is for Yaqui

Yaqui People were established along the Yaqui River by 552 CE their homeland was and remains, the Sonoran Desert which stretches across much of north-western Mexico and south-western USA. I had determined that I would restrict this overview of Native Americans to those living within the confines of what is now the United States even though such boundary did not exist until very late in the populating of the continent. So, why include the Yaqui? Their live style was typical of the indigenous people of the time; hunter/gathers with some cultivated crops like corn and squash. They traded with tribes as far to the north as the pueblo Zunis. The Spanish arrival in 1500 changed things, the Yaqui invited the Jesuit missionaries in and although they never got along with the Franciscans that later replaced them, they converted to Catholicism with a blend of their traditional religion thrown in. The Yaqui were in almost constant conflict with colonists and the Mexican government suffering enslavement, deportation and invasion of their lands. The "Yaqui Wars" which didn't end until 1929, brought on the bombing and strafing of their villages. Today the Yaqui maintain some degree of independence from the Mexican government. There are Yaqui districts in various cities throughout Mexico, the Mountain Yaqui were chased out of Sonora and now have a colony in Lubbock, Texas. There is a Yaqui Organization in Fresno, California whose motto is: "Yaqui and Proud." In Arizona, near Tucson, the Pascua Yaqui and the Yaqui of Guadalupe, near Tempe, known as a center of Yaqui culture, both settled by Yaquis fleeing Mexico, are Federally Recognized tribes that continue their unique blend of Christianity and traditional religion. Ceremonial leaders cross over from Mexico to ensure their ceremonies are held in correct accordance with the annual calendar. Pascua, Easter, the time of the Passion Play is a perfect example of the blending of Christian and Pre-Hispanic beliefs. Just as elsewhere in the world, Spring, the time of rebirth, renewal and revival for Pagans, fitted well with the theme of resurrection epitomized by the Passion of Jesus.

The most famous Yaqui, Don Juan de Matus, was introduced to the world by Carlos Castaneda in his book, *The Teachings of Don Juan: A Yaqui Way of Knowledge* for which Castaneda received his BA in Anthropology from UCLA. Castaneda met Don Juan in Arizona, he was so struck by the man that he went to Mexico and studied shamanism with him for several years. As noted elsewhere, anthropologists seldom agree about much but they mostly agreed on one thing, that Don Juan did not exist. This raises the question; would a student, rather than do proper field research, create a work of fiction and present it as his thesis to a board of Anthropologists at a prestigious University with the hope of fooling them into awarding him his BA? His only aim at the time. No one could have seen that it would become a best seller and that the series that followed would make Castaneda millions of dollars and influence millions of people. Sour grapes?

The Yaqui Pascola mask seen here is from, *Magic Faces, Caras Magicas* a collection of my Mexican mask paintings, with text in English and Spanish. The origin of the word Pascola is alternately given as coming from Pascua, Easter in Spanish, or from pahko'ola meaning "Old man of the ceremony."

"Pascolas are individuals who perform as a result of dreamed visions. Their knowledge is gained from animals of the woods, rather than from Christian supernaturals" (Fontana, Flaubert, Burn 1977)

Cool Fact: The Violence Against Women Act of 2013 (VAWA 2013) signed into law by President Barack Obama gives criminal jurisdiction by Indian tribal courts over non-Indian perpetrators of domestic violence that occur in Indian Country when the victim is Indian.

What other Tribal names start with Y?

ZUNI

Z is for Zuni

The Zuni, thought to be related to the Anazasi, settled on their land some 3-4000 years ago. They lived in typical Pueblo style adobe and rock houses. The discovery of the New World and the plunder Cortés reaped from the Aztecs inspired more exploration. One such expedition shipwrecked on Galveston Island, Texas, where the natives took them in and fed them. The expedition leader, Alvar Nuñez Cabeza de Vaca, an African slave, Estevánico and five others spent six years there before escaping. For two grueling years, they traveled through Texas, parts of New Mexico, and Arizona before entering Sonora where they met Spanish slavers. They finally arrived in Mexico City, July 24th, 1536. Near where El Paso now is, they were told of people further up the Rio Grande who lived in big towns with immense houses. Only four returned to Mexico but their tale of fabulous cities to the north led to a reconnaissance party under Fray Marcos de Niza, guided by Estevánico. Estevánico sent out Indian runners who reported of these great cities ahead which became known as the "Seven Cities of Cibola." The residents drew a line of corn flour on the earth and told the visitors not to cross it, Estevánico, still a slave but emboldened by his promotion to guide and the fact that he was the only one in the group who knew the way, crossed the line and was killed. Fray Marcos, some miles back, when told of Estevánico's death, fled back to Mexico with tales of a settlement larger than Tenochtitlán, The Aztec Capital, and a land, "larger and better than all those discovered." This was quite a stretch given that Tenochtitlán was far larger than any European city of the time. Nevertheless, another expedition under Francisco Vásquez de Coronado took off. Coronado was the next foreigner to see this "Cibola," they stormed the town and captured it in less than an hour although Coronado was seriously wounded. The shining city of gold was, in fact, Hawikuh, the largest of the Zuni Pueblos with six story adobe and rock buildings. Disappointed at the lack of gold, Coronado's party stole all the food they could find and went on to attack several other Pueblos. Still gullible, and anxious to find something to make the whole affair worthwhile, he was led on a wild goose chase looking for Quivira, another non-existent city of gold, before returning to Mexico empty handed. What followed for the Zuni was much the same as for other Pueblos, heavy-handed civilizing attempts by the invaders through the years resulting in rebellion and punishment. Today, the Zuni Pueblo, 40 some miles from Gallup, NM, is popular with those looking for Native American artwork. The Tribal Council estimates the production of turquoise and silver jewelry, pottery, basketry, bead-work, animal fetishes as well as other forms of artwork provides part of some 80% of all Zuni families' total income. Hawikuh is now a ruin on the National Historic Landmarks list and the Zunis live mostly in modest adobe, stucco or mobile homes. Though mostly Christian, their traditional religion and its ceremonies form the heart of Zuni life. The Zuni language, which has no relationship to any other Native American language, is taught in the schools for, as it was explained to me, "without our language we lose our history and our religion." Reconciling their innate conservatism with the need to provide work and a reason to stay on the reservation is something that occupies the tribal council and all those that wish to follow the Zuni way.

The Shalako dances and ceremonies, said to bring good fortune, abundant crops and many children, are conducted around the winter solstice. Newly built houses are blessed and thanks are given to the gods. It is a sacred drama that has been closed to non-natives since 1990. I was fortunate enough to see it and can attest to its powerful effect.

Cool Fact: Kokopelli a fertility deity, also associated with rain, usually depicted as a humpbacked, flute player often with a huge penis, is venerated by many tribes of the southwest USA, including the Zuni. The first known image dates from 750-850 CE. Unlike the Shalako, Kokopelli has crossed over, his image, minus the penis, can be found on T-shirts, ball caps, key-chains and any number of other objects.

What other Tribal names start with Z?

ISHI

Bonus
During an 1886 lecture, Theodore Roosevelt said, *"I don't go so far as to think that the only good Indians are dead Indians, but I believe nine out of ten are, and I shouldn't like to inquire too closely into the case of the tenth."* I'm sure that got a big laugh. As we have seen, this sentiment was not at all uncommon and deliberate efforts were carried out in order to see that there would be only 'good Indians.' There were many observers, those that were all for it and those that regretted it, who believed it was bound to come about. Native Americans fought against each other before and after white settlers arrived, they allied with the Dutch, the French, the Spanish and other Europeans against other tribes. Native Americans fought on both sides in the War of Independence and the American Civil War. Some owned slaves and helped the settlers enslave other tribes. Throughout time man has fought against man and committed the most inhumane crimes. Genocide shows no sign of going away. Is it inevitable, normal?

As noted elsewhere, it is not known just how many Native Americans there were on this continent before Columbus. European diseases spread across the land ahead of the invaders, wiping out entire peoples, leaving no record of their numbers, languages or history. Archaeologists, ethnologists and anthropologists attempt to reconstruct the past. It is estimated that there were 600 different languages, hundreds of distinct nations, any number of creation stories. Then followed the deliberate efforts to eradicate people with very little attempt to keep records of what or who they were. Some Native Americans were legislated out of existence; see the "one drop rule" of 1924. There are Federally recognized tribes and there are unrecognized groups seeking legitimization, while there are tribes that are classified as extinct, there are still plenty of people who claim to be descendants. The people exist, their tribe just isn't Federally recognized. Historical records present us with plenty of other examples. In 1835 the San Nicolas Island Indians were being transferred to the California mainland, a mother jumped overboard to go rescue her baby, left behind on the island. In 1853 she was found on the island, those that had been transferred were dead, as was her baby. She died a few months later without anyone being able to communicate with her. There is the case of Ishi, a Yahi indian whose life is chronicled in *Ishi in Two worlds* written by Theodora Kroeber, wife of the anthropologist Alfred L. Kroeber who, in 1911, with Thomas T. Waterman, having heard that a "wild Indian" had shown up near Oroville and was being held in a jail, arranged for him to be taken to the University of California's Anthropology Museum in San Francisco. With the help of some written Yana words and later, Sam Batwi, a Yana man, it was established that this 'wild man' was of the southernmost tribe of the Yana, the Yahi, whose language was similar. This was twenty years after the Yahi were thought to be extinct. Since one's name was only to be divulged to a relative or member of one's tribe, Ishi, 'man' in Yana, was the name Kroeber gave this relic of the past. His band had fled a massacre forty years earlier and lived totally isolated until all had died but for Ishi. At the museum Ishi demonstrated arrow making and numerous other crafts, recordings were made of him speaking, singing and telling stories. His mere presence drew crowds which he slowly learned to accept. During the next four years and seven months until his death, Ishi took his hosts back to his country where they photographed him reenacting his old life, he was invited to events, shopped in town and enjoyed his new life which included being a janitor at the museum. It was determined, many years later, that Ishi was of mixed Wintun or Nomlaki and Yahi blood. He may have been the last of his band and the last "wild man" but that mix meant he was not the last Yahi.

Cool Fact: In 1826 James Fenimore Cooper wrote *The Last of the Mohicans* a novel based on factual events in the past. His characters were modeled more on the Mohegan of Connecticut than the Mohican of upstate New York. Like many others, Cooper believed that the Native Americans were doomed to become extinct. It was not the last of the Mohicans, however. Their language may be extinct but, The Stockbridge-Munsee Band of Mohican Indians are doing well, operating their resort and casino on the reservation.

In Beauty May I walk

With beauty may I walk.
With beauty before me, may I walk.
With beauty behind me, may I walk.
With beauty above me, may I walk.
With beauty below me, may I walk.
With beauty all around me, may I walk.

It is finished in beauty.
It is finished in beauty.
It is finished in beauty.
It is finished in beauty.

Excerpt from a version of the Navajo Night Chant.

Other Tribal Names

A. Apache, Algonquin, Arapaho, Arikawa, Aztec

B. Big Valley Band of Pomo.

C. Cahuilla, Cherokee, Cheyenne, Chippewa, Comanche, Cree, Crow

D. Dakota, Delaware

E. Erie, Eyeish, Eno

F. Fox, Fremont, Fernandeno

G. Gila, Guale, Guasas, Guacata

H. Huron, Ho-Chunk, Havasupi, Hupa

I. Iroquis, Iowa, Illinois

J. Jemez, Jamui,

K. Kickapoo, Klamath, Kumeyaay

L. Lakota, Laguna. Lenape,

M. Modoc, Mohawk, Muscogee, Miami, Meskwaki, Micmac

N. Nez Perce, Nooksack

O. Odawa, Omaha, Oneida, Ottawa, Otoe

P. Pawnee, Ponca, Pima, Potawatomi

Q. Quapaw, Quinault, Quechan

R. Raritan, Ramona

S. Shoshone, Shawnee, Sauk, Shinnecock

T. Tonkawa, Tohono-O'odham, Tuscarora, Tawakoni, Tuskigee

U. Ucita, Upper Skagit Tribe of Washington, unrecognized tribesmen

V. Venetie Tribal Government of Alaska, Virgin Island Opia Carib Tribe

W. Wichita, Winnebago, Washoe, Wyandotte

X.

Y. Yurok, Ysleta Del Sur Pueblo,

Z. Zia

Bibliography

Catlin, George. Edited by Peter Matthiessen. *North American Indians.* Penguin Books, 1989.

Newcomb, W.W. *The Indians of Texas.* University of Texas at Austin, 1961.

Utley, Robert & Washburn, Wilcomb. *The Indian Wars.* American Heritage Publishing, 1977.

Mysteries of the Ancient Americans. Readers Digest Inc., 1986.

Weatherford, Jack. *Indian Givers*. Ballantine Books, N.Y., 1988.

Nansen, Fridjof 1893. *Eskimo Life* Longmans, Green & Co., 1893.

Warner, John Anson. *The Life & Art of the North American Indian* Chartwell Books, N. J., 1990.

Hillerman, Tony. Photography by Béla Kalman. *Indian Country* Northland Press, 1987.

Sturtevant, William, Editor. *Handbook of North American Indians* Smithsonian Institute, Washington, DC, 1978.

Tedlock, Dennis and Barbara, Editors. *Teachings from the American Earth* Liveright, New York, 1975.

Josephy, Alvin M. Jr. *500 Nations* Alfred A. Knopf, New York, 1994.

Mather, Christine. Photography by Jack Parsons. *Native America* Clarkson N.Potter, Inc., 1990.

Shafer, Harry J. *Ancient Texans* Texas Monthly Press, Austin, Tx., 1986.

Kroeber, Theodora. *Ishi in Two Worlds* University of California Press, 1961.

Ostler, Jeffrey 2020. *Surviving Genocide: Native Americans and the United States from the American Revolution to Bleeding Kansas.* Yale University Press, 2020.

Winegard, Timothy C. *The Mosquito: A Human History of Our Deadliest Predator* Dutton, 2020

archaeology.org.

Youtube

Wikipedia

The Canadian Encyclopedia

www.encyclopedia.com

Running Strong for American Indian Youth.

Various Tribal websites